Practice and Theory of Tibetan Buddhism

Practice and Theory of Tibetan Buddhism

GESHE LHUNDUP SOPA
AND JEFFREY HOPKINS

With a Foreword by
His Holiness The Dalai Lama

GROVE PRESS, INC.
NEW YORK

ISBN: 0-394-17905-6
Grove Press ISBN: 0-8021-4006-8
Library of Congress Catalog Card Number: 75-42898
First Evergreen Edition 1976
First Printing
Manufactured in the United States of America

Distributed by Random House, Inc., New York

GROVE PRESS, INC., 196 West Houston Street, New York, N.Y. 10014

CONTENTS

THE DALAI LAMA

THEKCHEN CHOELING
DHARMSALA CANTT
KANGRA DISTRICT
HIMACHAL PRADESH

FOREWORD

Buddhahood - the state of being a source of help and happiness for all sentient beings - is attained through method and wisdom. The chief method is the altruistic aspiration to highest enlightenment for the sake of all sentient beings, and the chief wisdom is the correct view of emptiness - the realization that phenomena do not exist in their own right.

An altruistic aspiration to highest enlightenment is induced by love and compassion which are in turn induced by applying knowledge of one's own plight in cyclic existence to others. It is first necessary to realize the manifold sufferings of cyclic existence, both the obvious, such as physical and mental pain resulting from war, and the non-obvious, such as the mere fact of having a mind and body which are so composed that the aggregation of secondary circumstances will create immense pain.

Realizing that one's own wish to avoid suffering and attain happiness is shared equally with all sentient beings, one can generate love - the wish that all sentient beings have happiness - and compassion - the wish that all sentient beings be free from suffering. It is possible, in turn, even to generate the motivation of a Bodhisattva wherein one assumes alone the burden of the welfare of all beings, from the tiniest insects upwards. A Bodhisattva then seeks Buddhahood as a means toward the primary goal of helping others.

To achieve Buddhahood the afflictions of desire, hatred, and ignorance as well as the predispositions that they establish in the mind must be overcome. The means to do this are the realization of and subsequent prolonged meditation on emptiness - the non-inherent existence of each and every phenomenon, from forms through to omniscient consciousness.

2/-

Within Buddhist schools the views of emptiness or selflessness are presented in many ways, with the lower systems serving as means of penetrating the higher views. One gradually learns the compatibility of dependent-arising and emptiness and eventually can generate a wisdom consciousness capable not just of temporarily supressing the afflictions but of removing forever the inborn misconception of the nature of phenomena which provides a false foundation for the afflictions. By understanding that phenomena do not inherently exist but exist only nominally or imputedly, it becomes possible to develop the mind fully and thereby spontaneously effect the welfare of countless beings.

The two treatises in this volume - by the Fourth Panchen Lama and Kon-chok-jik-may-wang-po - together with the supplementary commentaries should help to provide an understanding of the structure of this path.

Tenzin Gyatso
THE XIVTH DALAI LAMA

August 30, 1974

PREFACE

Homage to Mañjuśrī

This book offers an insight into the practical and theoretical aspects of Tibetan Buddhism. Part One epitomizes much of the daily practice of Tibetan monks and yogīs. Though the text is taken from the Gelukpa order of Tibetan Buddhism, it typifies in many ways the practice of all Tibetan orders, Nyingmapa, Kagyupa, Sakyapa, and Gelukpa. The treatise was written by the Fourth Panchen Lama (1781–1852/4) as a commentary to a short verse letter by Tsong-ka-pa on the three principal aspects of the path to highest enlightenment.

Part Two presents a solid introduction both to the theory behind the practice and the theory being realized in practice. This treatise, which is also taken from Gelukpa commentary, presents a map of the entire spectrum of the Buddhist schools of tenets. Providing a student with a basis for continuing study of Buddhist philosophy, it details the presentations of cyclic existence and selflessness in the four schools, Vaibhāṣika, Sautrāntika, Cittamātra, and Mādhyamika. The text was written by Kön-chok-jik-may-wang-po (dKon-mchog-'jigs-med-dbang-po, 1728–91), the reincarnation of Jam-yang-shay-ba ('Jam-byangs-bzhad-pa), author of the textbook literature for the Gomang College of Drepung Monastery in Lhasa.

In Part One extensive portions of the six preparatory practices only mentioned in the text are given in full. Also, two stanzas of Tsong-ka-pa's basic text, omitted by the Panchen Lama, have been restored. Tsong-ka-pa's verse letter, which forms the basic text for the Fourth Panchen Lama's commentary, is set in italics.

In Part One the material in square brackets has been added by the translators to facilitate understanding. In Part Two short comments by the translators have been similarly set in brackets, with longer commentary in separate paragraphs of smaller type.

We wish to express a debt of gratitude to the late Professor Richard Robinson and to Professor Harvey Aronson for making many suggestions that improved the English of Part One. We particularly wish to express our thanks to Anne Klein for providing the impetus for us to recast our translation of Part Two, the presentation of tenets, and to add commentary so that it might be more accessible. She helped not only to edit that part but also to compile the glossary and index.

GESHE LHUNDUP SOPA
JEFFREY HOPKINS

INTRODUCTION AND COMMENTS ON THE TEXT OF PART ONE

Part One is a meditation manual; it details how to prepare for and how to conduct a meditative session. It is highly practical with nothing said that does not fit directly into an actual meditation. It does not describe the levels of trance, the hindrances to meditation and their antidotes, or the powers of mind present at various levels of meditation. It elaborates only on those points which are directly applicable to the format of a session. The proofs for emptiness are not explained in detail, but how to meditate on emptiness is explained. The proofs for impermanence are not explained in detail, but meditation on renunciation of the impermanent and miserable is explained.

Therefore, it is imperative that readers new to Buddhism seek other works of instruction on doctrinal matters. They will find that Part Two of this book, a translation and explanation of Kön-chok-jik-may-wang-po's *Precious Garland of Tenets*, supplements the manual and in no way contradicts the explicit or implicit import of the instructions given. For the practice of Tibetan Buddhism is founded on a thorough study of Buddhist theory, the practices being a means of internalizing theory to the point where it becomes spontaneous.

The mind does not of its own course, unless it has been trained, abide in the right path due to beginningless conditioning to the three poisons of desire, hatred, and ignorance. Therefore, practice is necessary. In the beginning practice is always artificial unless, through training in a previous lifetime, one's predispositions are awakened upon contacting the material again and the attitudes sought arise of their own force. However, for most, the beginning is a matter of hard conditioning to new ideas, and thus frequent repetition is necessary.

This manual gives in complete detail the instructions necessary for daily practice. A yogī would perform the whole meditation at least once and at most four times a day. However, the beginning student often finds that it takes considerable time to become acquainted with each phase of the meditation, and thus he only concentrates on a certain phase of the session until he gains a minimal familiarity. A beginner also tends to limit meditation to short periods of from ten to twenty minutes in order to avoid lethargy or undue excitement.

Even though an aim is to perform the more complicated visualizations in all their detail, it is impossible for a beginner, who must use the technique of pretending to conduct the full visualization. This acts as a cause of actually being able to do it fully in the future.

Any persons outside the tradition who attempt such meditation are cautioned to beware of entering into difficult meditation without the proper preparation in terms of motivation and theory. One of the goals is to develop flexibility of mind, and if a student begins to become rigid, he is advised to identify the mispractice and seek a means of alleviating the problem. Thus, any who newly seek to practise this text are to be cautioned that the advice of a skilful teacher is often necessary.

Comments on the text

This Tibetan meditation manual was written by the fourth Panchen Lama, Lo-sang-pel-den-ten-pay-nyi-ma (bLo-bzang-dpal-ldan-bstan-pa'i-nyi-ma, 1781–1852/4) and is based on an epistolary verse essay by Tsong-ka-pa (1357–1419). Tsong-ka-pa was condensing the import of Buddha's *sūtras* in a short letter to his student, Tsa-ko-pön-po (Tsha-kho-dpon-po), to whom he affectionately refers as 'son' in the last word of the poem. The Panchen Lama's text is not a commentary of notes or a commentary on the difficult points of Tsong-ka-pa's work. Rather, it is intended for practice. Tsong-ka-pa's work is called *The*

Three Principal Aspects of the Path to Highest Enlightenment, and the main part of the commentary is concerned with the internalization of these three principal factors of the path: the thought definitely to leave cyclic existence, the aspiration to enlightenment for the sake of all sentient beings, and the correct view of emptiness. It is preceded by preliminary practices and followed by concluding practices. This is the basic structure of the book and of the meditation discussed.

These three principal aspects of the path are the essence of all the nearly countless scriptures of Buddha and their commentaries, and thus meditation based on them is not to be seen as merely partial or merely introductory. Tsong-ka-pa's book and the Panchen's commentary are both written from the point of view of the Mahāyāna and, within that, the highest of the philosophical schools, the Mādhyamika-Prāsaṅgika. The book details the practices which are common requirements for both the *sūtra* and *tantra* paths. Though there are tantric practices which are considered to be 'higher' than those presented here, all of them require these three principals as prerequisites and none of them at any time forsakes these three. The thought definitely to leave cyclic existence is renunciation, and this is as essential to the practice of *tantra* as it is to that of *sūtra*; in *tantra* the discipline is even stricter than that of the *sūtra* systems. The aspiration to enlightenment for the sake of all sentient beings is the assumption of the burden of freeing all sentient beings from misery and joining them with happiness and the consequent wish for Buddhahood, the state wherein one has the power to effect the promise to free all beings. It forms the motivation for *tantra* practice as well as for *sūtra* practice. The correct view is the realization of emptiness, the realization that all phenomena do not exist inherently, are just imputations by thought, nominally existent and effective but not to be found under analysis. Emptiness itself is the life of *sūtra* and *tantra*.

What some *tantras* have that this text does not are certain difficult and dangerous practices for highly trained yogīs to achieve in a very short time the aim of Buddhahood. Thus, undoubtedly the Panchen Lama chose Tsong-ka-pa's text for his basis because it provides the essentials of the path to Buddhahood and is not limited in scope to practices which aim at temporary beneficial results such as rebirths in higher realms.

Tsong-ka-pa received the precepts on the three principal aspects of the path from Mañjughoṣa, or Mañjuśrī, himself. Through devotion and meditation Tsong-ka-pa attained a meeting with Mañjuśrī, and this the Panchen Lama offers as recommendation for the book's reliability and great worth.

The manual begins with instructions on how to prepare for the actual meditation on the three principal aspects of the path to enlightenment. The preparations given are common throughout Tibetan Buddhism, not just for the particular meditation of this book, but for any meditation. They are called the six preparatory practices:

1. Cleansing the place where one is meditating in order to receive a visit from Buddha and arranging on an altar an image of Buddha, a scripture, and for instance a reliquary (*stūpa*) to symbolize the body, speech, and mind of Buddha.

2. Arranging offerings which are procured honestly: water, food, clothing, and so forth.

3. Positioning one's own body. The posture recommended has seven features:

(*a*) Sitting on a soft and comfortable cushion in the lotus or half-lotus position.

(*b*) Keeping the eyes neither opened very wide nor closed tight, aimed at the point of the nose. One should avoid looking hard at the point of the nose, but should set the gaze there gently.

(*c*) Keeping the body straight with the backbone like a pile of coins.

(*d*) Keeping the shoulders level.

(*e*) Keeping the head neither high nor low, unmovingly in a straight line from the nose to the navel.

(*f*) Setting the teeth and lips as usual with the tongue set against the back of the upper teeth.

(*g*) Breathing quietly and gently.

It is said that if one leans forward, ignorance is increased; if to the right, jealousy; if to the left, desire; if to the back, pride. Thus the proper posture is important.

After positioning the body, the field of assembly of the Buddha, Bodhisattvas, one's own teachers, and so forth, is visualized in front of oneself. The motivation for taking refuge is reflected on. One is concerned with the sufferings of all ordinary beings in cyclic existence. One is concerned with their turning to a religion of utter solitary peace perfecting neither their own nor others' aims. One is concerned with the afflictions which obstruct them from liberation from cyclic existence and with the obstructions which prevent them from simultaneously cognizing all phenomena. Realizing that the Three Jewels have the power to protect all beings from these four ills, one then takes refuge, asking for help for all beings.

Refuge is taken in Buddha as the teacher of refuge, in the Doctrine as the actual refuge, principally in the sense of the true cessation of all afflictions, or *nirvāṇa*, and in the Spiritual Community as helpers toward refuge.

Rather than leaving the taking of refuge just as a petition, the manual instructs the meditator to simulate the actual aid of the Three Jewels for all sentient beings through visualizing ambrosia falling from their bodies. With the statement of one's intention to attain Buddhahood in order to help all sentient beings, the deities visualized in front of oneself are pleased and send a duplicate of themselves into the meditator. One suddenly turns into the lama and Buddha and thereupon performs the aiding of all beings through emanating from one's body a light that strikes and purifies all beings, establishing them in Buddhahood.

This type of practice is particularly tantric in that one is not just aspiring to Buddhahood but is actualizing while still on the path the condition of Buddhahood itself. Just as one does not consider the beings visualized in front of oneself to be just visualizations or figments of imagination but the real Refuges themselves, so one considers that one has actually for the moment become a Buddha. Because this technique is based on simulating the eventual effect of practice, the *tantra* system is called effect. The *sūtra* system, based in many of its practices on developing aspirations for the effect, is called cause. This manual is a mixture of the two systems.

To establish the motivation for meditating on the three principal aspects of the path, the text calls for cultivation of the four immeasurables. These are: equanimity, love, compassion, and joy; they are 'immeasurable' because the field with respect to which one is meditating is the infinite field of all sentient beings throughout all space. Each of the four immeasurables passes through three stages of heightening force. The first is a statement of how nice it would be if all sentient beings had equanimity, happiness, freedom from suffering, and high status and the bliss of liberation. The second is the wish that they may come to have these. The third is to take upon oneself the burden of causing all sentient beings to have these. Only Bodhisattvas have the third; however, the Hīnayāna Hearers do have the other two, and thus it is said that they have limitless compassion or even great compassion. However, they do not have the great compassion that involves taking upon oneself the burden of freeing all sentient beings from suffering and joining all sentient beings with happiness.

The wish to free all without exception from suffering and the causes of suffering is mercy or compassion, and the wish to join all without exception with happiness and the causes of happiness is love. In contrast worldly love and mercy are limited in the scope of the objects of attention; all persons are not valued similarly; some are considered to be close and some distant.

Having stated that he will free all beings from suffering and establish all beings in happiness, the meditator states his determination to attain Buddhahood in order to carry out his intentions. The full development of this thought is *bodhicitta*, the aspiration to highest enlightenment for the sake of all sentient beings. With this motivation one enters into cultivation of the three principal aspects of the path to highest enlightenment.

4. Visualization of the field of assembly of the great teachers and masters of Buddhism is the fourth of the six preparatory practices. An important part of the meditation is an invitation to the actual deities to dissolve into the visualized beings. One drops

all consideration of them as just visualizations, ceases any thought that they are actually somewhere else, and views these visualizations as the real beings themselves.

5. Performance of the seven branches of practice together with offering *maṇḍalas* is done through recitation of verses from the *Prayers of Samantabhadra*. The seven parts are:

(*a*) Obeisance (*phyag 'tshal ba*)
(*b*) Offering (*mchod pa*)
(*c*) Revealing one's own faulty deeds (*bshags pa*)
(*d*) Admiring one's own and others' virtues (*rjes su yi rang*)
(*e*) Entreaty (*bskul ba*)
(*f*) Supplication (*gsol ba*)
(*g*) Dedication (*bsngo ba*).

The offering of *maṇḍala* involves offering the purified world system together with sun and moon and all imaginable marvels to the field of assembly.

6. The last practice of preparation is supplication to the lineage of gurus of the principal aspects of the path for aid in generating the proper attitudes and understanding.

When Buddha was about to die, he was asked by his attendants on whom they should rely after his death. His answer was that he would enter any teacher whom they believed to be an actual Buddha whereupon the teacher then would be equal to Buddha. An aim of this practice is to bring the highest value to the teaching which one receives through not imagining that Buddha and a better teaching are available elsewhere.

In order to practise the teaching it is necessary to have leisure and fortune. Leisure means to be free from the eight conditions of non-leisure:

1. birth as a hell-being
2. birth as a hungry ghost
3. birth as an animal
4. birth in an uncultured area
5. possessing defective sense faculties
6. having wrong views

7. birth as a god of long life
8. birth in a world system where a Buddha did not come.

Fortune means the five inner fortunes:

1. being a human
2. being born in a centre of Buddhist teaching
3. having sound sense faculties
4. not having done the five actions of immediate retribution in a hell after death: killing one's father, killing one's mother, killing a Foe Destroyer, with bad intention causing blood to flow from the body of a Buddha, and causing dissension in the Spiritual Community
5. having faith in Buddha's scriptures.

Fortune also means the five outer fortunes:

1. a visitation from a Buddha
2. his teaching the excellent Doctrine
3. his teaching remaining to the present
4. his followers still existing
5. the people of the area having mercy and love for others and thus teaching others.

Thus, a life of complete leisure and fortune precludes being anything other than a human. For, even the gods of the desire realm, though very happy, are lured by that happiness into complacency; therefore, one is exhorted to accumulate, while a human, the causes of happiness, the ten virtues which are the avoidance of the ten non-virtues:

1. killing
2. stealing
3. sexual misconduct
4. lying
5. divisive talk
6. harsh speech
7. foolish talk
8. covetousness
9. harmfulness
10. wrong ideas.

The first three are physical; the middle four are verbal; and the last three are mental. One is exhorted to desist from these as much as possible because the effects of even tiny non-virtues can be very great. A moment of anger toward a Bodhisattva can destroy the virtue accumulated over a thousand aeons. Similarly, a moment of strong contrition can destroy the non-virtues of aeons. Cause and effect which are associated with the mind are said to be unlike cause and effect in the external world. Though a great oak tree grows out of an acorn, far, far greater effects in terms of intensity and duration are produced from deeds due to the importance of motivation.

Cyclic existence is a mass of suffering. Even the happiest beings in the desire realm are in a state of suffering. When the gods die, they face with a special 'clairvoyance' the horrors that are to come. They also perceive five signs of their approaching death:

1. dust gathering around the body
2. sweat coming from the armpits
3. fading of their garlands of flowers
4. body beginning to smell
5. discomfort with the environment.

The force of the actions which caused those beings to be born as gods ceases, and having exhausted great funds of good action, they are forced into lower rebirths. Humans, on the other hand, often have enough suffering to spur them into practice and sufficient leisure to be able to achieve results. Unlike animals, humans can begin new practices of virtue. Thus, human life is a rare and precious phenomenon which must be used meaningfully. The practice of virtues should at least be aimed at rebirth in a happy migration so that one can continue religious practice in order to be freed entirely from cyclic existence.

The two wings of the bird flying to Buddhahood are wisdom and compassion. Without the full development of compassion to the point where one takes upon oneself the burden of liberating all sentient beings from suffering and establishing them in happiness, a yogī can only attain the fruit of a Hearer (*Śrāvaka*) or Solitary Realizer (*Pratyekabuddha*). Thus, after cultivating the wish to leave cyclic existence due to its misery, one extends through inference what one now knows about one's own condition to that of others and develops the wish to free all beings from suffering.

The yogī is directed to generate *bodhicitta*. *Bodhicitta* in general is of two types: ultimate and conventional. The ultimate *bodhicitta* is a Buddha's or Bodhisattva's wisdom of emptiness; it is the sign of the Bodhisattva's attainment of the path of seeing, the time of initially cognizing emptiness directly. Emptiness is realized earlier through inference, but this is the first direct cognition. From this point on, whenever the Bodhisattva directly cognizes emptiness, his mental consciousness is an ultimate *bodhicitta*. The conventional *bodhicitta* is of two types: one is the aspiration to highest enlightenment for the sake of all sentient beings and the other is that aspiration conjoined with the Bodhisattva deeds.

The *bodhicitta* being generated in the second part of the actual meditation is the aspirational conventional *bodhicitta*, and thus it has here been translated as 'the aspiration to enlightenment' often adding 'for the sake of all sentient beings'. For its generation there are seven precepts of cause and effect:

1. recognition of all sentient beings as one's mothers
2. becoming mindful of their kindness
3. promising to repay their kindness
4. love
5. great compassion
6. the unusual attitude
7. generation of the aspiration to Buddhahood for the sake of all beings.

The lineage of this system of practice extends from Śākyamuni Buddha to Maitreya to Asaṅga. The aim is to extend a sense of intimacy and closeness to all beings without exception. Nonpartiality is what distinguishes pure love from worldly love. Worldly love is always partial.

The relationship with one's mother is used as the model because of the mother's extremely great kindness and devotion. Upon consideration, it was one's mother who taught one as a child to walk, talk, take sustenance, and so forth. Without this teaching it is said that we would resemble bugs—helplessly incommunicative. In Buddhism an offspring is to feel thankful to his parents for their protection, sustenance, and teaching. It is wrong to feel that parents somehow owe a good life to their offspring because they created him. Rather, the act of copulation of the parents provided a suitable home for one's consciousness which was in the intermediate state, after death and before rebirth. In comparison with many other modes and types of birth one can only be thankful for what the parents have done. Any troubles that are encountered are created through the fructification of one's own former ill deeds. That fructification should be accepted without compounding the problem by creating new ill will.

Lamas often advise those who have difficulty reflecting on the kindness of the mother to set aside for the moment the tangle of bad thoughts and concentrate for the moment on her kindness and the marvellous protection and love which she afforded. If the relationship with one's mother is either not clear or too complicated, they advise that one use the relationship with one's closest friend as the model.

The final generation of the aspiration to enlightenment is the seventh stage of the seven cause and effect precepts. The yogī now is firm in his resolve to take upon himself the burden of freeing all beings, and he reflects on whether he has the ability to do so. Realizing that he has difficulty even knowing what he is doing, he sees that only a completely perfect Buddha has such ability. He ascertains that he must attain Buddhahood.

It is said that those of very sharp intellect first ascertain that Buddhahood would be the best means of helping others and then, before they pass on to the resolve to attain Buddhahood, reflect on whether the mind can be so purified that Buddhahood actually is possible. They realize that the mind is like a crystal which has become dirty and that the dirt can be cleaned away without destroying the crystal. In other words, they realize through inference the emptiness of the mind; they realize that the afflicted mind does not naturally exist but is produced from causes and conditions and thus is capable of being changed. They thereby ascertain that it is possible to attain Buddhahood. Then they make a resolve to attain Buddhahood. When *bodhicitta* is produced in this manner it is called a gold-like generation of the aspiration to highest enlightenment. For, just as gold is 'unchangeable', so the Bodhisattva will never fall from his aspiration.

The generation of the conventional *bodhicitta* is the beginning of the Bodhisattva path of accumulation. For three countless aeons he accumulates the stocks of merit and wisdom, especially practising the six perfections. He also practises all six perfections in each perfection. For example, he performs the giving of giving, the ethics of giving, the patience of giving, the effort of giving, the concentration of giving, and the wisdom of giving; similarly, he performs the giving of ethics, the ethics of ethics, and so forth, totalling thirty-six. The wisdom of giving refers to the realization that giver, giving, gift, and receiver do not exist inherently or truly but are imputedly existent. This means that under analysis the giver and so forth cannot be found, but this does not mean that the giver is utterly non-existent or that giving need not be practised. Rather, one strongly practises giving within the context of realizing the merely nominal existence of agent, action and object.

In order to cut out the root of cyclic existence, it is necessary to realize emptiness, first conceptually through inference and then in a totally non-dualistic direct cognition. Emptiness in the highest Buddhist philosophical system, the Prāsaṅgika, is the lack of inherent existence, true existence, natural existence, existence in its own right, or real existence. This means that objects are only imputed to bases of imputation. For instance, 'chair' is imputed to a collection of four legs, a back, and a seat, but 'chair' is not any one of those parts individually, nor is it separate from those parts, nor is it the collection of those parts. If 'chair' were the collection of the parts of the chair, it would mean that each part was a chair or that the collection had no parts. Therefore, a chair exists only imputedly or by designation.

It is undeniable that phenomena appear *to be* their basis of imputation, that a chair appears *to be* the collection of its parts;

however, this appearance, even to a sense consciousness, is wrong. It must be rooted out first with respect to the 'person' and then with respect to other phenomena through searching analytically in meditation to find the 'person' or 'chair' and discovering that they cannot be found among their bases of imputation.

First it is necessary to see clearly what is being negated in the theory of selflessness. Selflessness does not negate something that is existent; rather it shows that something which is misconceived to exist does not exist. Thus, though true existence or inherent existence does not exist, a concept or image of true existence, its conception, and its conceiver do exist. The first step in meditation on the personal selflessness is to see this truly existent or independent or self-sufficient self as it appears to our ordinary non-analytical intellect. One technique is to calm the mind, sit very quietly, and then think 'I' and observe what happens. Another is to watch oneself when being falsely accused to see the sense of a self-sufficient 'I' that is generated and forms the centre of one's response.

The inborn, habitual, or innate misconception of a self is distinguished from the imputed or learned misconception of a self. The latter is a misconception acquired through false teachings, scriptures, and proofs. The innate misconception, however, requires no teaching; it is the result of beginningless conditioning. The way that the inborn misconception of a self apprehends the person is difficult to express concisely. The person is not perceived as if it were entirely separate from the mental and physical aggregates; for instance, when some part of the body, such as the stomach, is ill, we think, 'I am sick', seemingly identifying the self with the stomach. However, the 'I' is also not perceived as if it were completely the same as the aggregates. For example, if we see a particularly handsome person, we are apt to think, 'I might be like that', feeling even to exchange bodies with the person, whereas if we were utterly the same as our body, we could not even imagine such a thing. The 'I' as perceived by the inborn conceiver of a self is to our own sight neither completely the same as nor completely different from the aggregates. Still, an appearance of a seemingly self-sufficient 'I' can and must be seen in order to identify what must be destroyed. It will be replaced with the unadulterated conception of the person as imputed dependent on the mind and body but not findable either among or separate from the mind and body.

Similarly, the appearance of a self-sufficient body is described as a 'whole, looming body' with 'looming' having the sense of a big black thing seen in the dark which turns out to be nothing. The body of flesh and bone is described in the same sentence as 'bubbly', meaning that just as bubbles appear to be substantial phenomena but are seen to be destroyed quickly, so are flesh and bone. Also, just as bubbles come up and grow out from the water, flesh and bone grow out into lumps. What is being investigated is whether something with parts is itself a whole or whether its wholeness is just designated to it. Further, since each part is a whole, it is to be seen that parts are only imputedly existent. The theory is that all ordinary perceptions are misinformed about the nature of the object; things appear to exist inherently but do not. Through conditioning to emptiness these misconceptions and false perceptions can be utterly eliminated.

Eventually a yogī becomes so skilled that perception of appearances aids him in understanding emptiness, for he understands that objects exist only imputedly and not inherently. This absence of inherent existence is emptiness. Also, reflection on emptiness aids him in understanding appearances, for emptiness is the negative of inherent existence and not of nominal existence. Thus, appearances keep him away from the extreme of existence, and emptiness keeps him away from the extreme of non-existence. This indicates the high degree of skill required in delimiting just what is denied in the theory of emptiness, just inherent existence and not nominal existence.

Emptinesses are ultimate truths or highest object truths (*paramārtha-satya*) because they are the objects of the highest wisdom and because they appear in direct cognition exactly the way they are. All other phenomena (*dharma*), permanent and impermanent, are truths for a concealer (*saṃvṛti-satya*) because an ignorant consciousness, the concealer of the reality of emptiness through conceiving things to exist inherently, assumes they exist the way they appear. In other words, in direct perception all objects except emptinesses falsely appear to exist inherently and not just to exist imputedly, unfindable among their bases of imputation. Ignorance, here specifically the misapprehender of the nature of things, takes these appearances to be correct. Therefore, conventional objects are said to be truths with respect to ignorance.

This means that ignorance falsely establishes the inherent existence of objects; it does not mean that ignorance establishes the existence of objects. For all phenomena conventionally exist validly (*pramāṇa-siddha*). It is their mode of existence that has been misinterpreted, and this is one reason why the phenomena of the universe are divided into the two truths: to show that for non-Buddhas conventional objects—all things except emptinesses—are truths only for ignorance. They do not exist the way they appear. One is called to search for emptiness, the object of the highest wisdom.

The session concludes with a dedication. One is seeking through the dedication never to become separated from the two stages of *tantra* and the four wheels of the Mahāyāna. The two stages of *tantra* are:

1. the stage of producing the ripening of the mental continuum from ordinary to exalted perceptions through imagining oneself as a deity and one's environment as the habitation of a deity
2. the stage of completing the wisdom of the non-differentiation of emptiness and bliss, and one's actually becoming a deity.

The four wheels of the Mahāyāna are:

1. living in a place where the necessities for practising the Mahāyāna are easily found
2. relying on a holy being who practises and teaches the Mahāyāna
3. having great aspirations for the practice of the Mahāyāna
4. having produced great merit in the past.

The purpose of seeking to remain with the Mahāyāna is that through practice of it Buddhahood can be achieved, and having the powers of a Buddha, one will be able to help others. Therefore the dedication at the conclusion of the session is aimed toward one's own enlightenment for the sake of all sentient beings. It is said that because the field of dedication is so vast—all sentient beings—the virtue of the session cannot be lost. Often the benefits of practice are lost through periods of anger, but through dedicating the virtue of the session for the sake of all sentient beings the benefits are never lost, surviving even anger. Thus, upon finishing any virtuous activity it is important to dedicate it immediately toward the enlightenment of Buddhahood which alone enables one to help all sentient beings.

PART ONE

Practice: Meditation in Tibetan Buddhism

A translation of the Fourth Panchen Lama's *Instructions on [Tsong-ka-pa's] 'Three Principal Aspects of the Path', the Essence of All the Scriptures, the Quintessence of Helping Others*

This Part has three overriding divisions: preparation for a session (Chapter I), the actual session (Chapters II to V), and the conclusion of a session (Chapter VI).

I. PREPARATION FOR THE SESSION

Oṃ svasti. I bow down and go for refuge to the feet of the excellent holy lamas who have great compassion. I pray to be taken care of by them at all times with great love.

This is a book of practices concerning the instructions on the three principal aspects of the path which are the extraordinary precepts actually bestowed by the protector Mañjughoṣa on the great Tsong-ka-pa, the King of Doctrine of the three realms. It contains the essential meanings of all the scriptures of the Conqueror Buddha with commentary, collected in stages of practice for individuals. It details the two systems: how to act in the actual session of meditation and how to act between sessions.

PREPARATION

Perform, for instance, the six practices of preparation:

Clean well the room where you are practising. Second, beautifully arrange offerings [procured] without deceit. Third, on a comfortable cushion assume a posture having the seven features of Vairocana['s way of sitting]. Then, with respect to generating an attitude of refuge and so forth from within a special, virtuous attitude, the objects of refuge should first be set clearly [in front of you in visualization]:

Directly in front of you there is a high and broad throne of jewels raised up by eight great lions. On that, on cushions of the spheres of variegated lotus and sun and moon, is your kind, fundamental lama in actuality but in the form of the Conqueror Śākyamuni with pure gold body, his head having the crown protrusion. His right hand presses the earth [in the gesture of calling the goddess of the earth to witness his achievement]. His left hand, in the pose of meditative equipoise, carries a bowl filled with ambrosia. He is wearing the saffron religious robes. A mass of light is generated from his body, which is adorned with the major and minor marks and has a nature of pure, clear light. In the middle of the mass of light he sits with his two legs in the adamantine posture. Surrounding him are sitting collections of your actual and indirect lamas, deities, Buddhas, Bodhisattvas, Heroes, Sky-Goers, and Protectors of Doctrine. On marvellous tables in front of each of them are the verbal doctrines taught by each in the form of books having the nature of light.

The members of the field of assembly are pleased with you. Abiding in the greatest faith, mindful of the virtues and kindness of the field of assembly, think:

I and all sentient beings, the mothers, from beginningless time until now have undergone various sufferings of cyclic existence in general and of the three bad migrations in particular. However, it is still difficult to comprehend the depth and limits of suffering.

Now I have attained the special body of a human which has leisure and fortune, is difficult to find and, if found, is extremely meaningful. If at this time of meeting with Buddha's precious teaching I do not attain the state of completely perfect Buddhahood, the supreme liberation that eradicates all suffering, I must again undergo the suffering at least of cyclic existence in general and perhaps also of the three bad migrations in particular.

The power of protection from these sufferings exists in the lamas and the Three Jewels, who are sitting in front of me. I will attain the state of perfect Buddhahood for the sake of all sentient beings, the mothers. In order to do so, I will go for refuge to the lamas and the Three Jewels.

I go for refuge to the Lamas. I go for refuge to the Buddhas. I go for refuge to the Doctrine. I go for refuge to the Spiritual Community.

Recite the abridged refuge, 'I go for refuge until perfect enlightenment to Buddha, the Doctrine, and Supreme Community.' Think:

From the bodies of all the objects of refuge, a stream of the five kinds of ambrosia [white, red, blue, yellow, and green] together with rays of light is falling and entering the bodies and minds of all sentient beings, myself and others. It is purifying all sickness, possession [i.e madness], sins, and obstructions with their latencies beginninglessly accumulated. It is developing and furthering merits, life-span, and all the qualities of verbal and cognitive understanding. In particular, it also is purifying the sins, obstructions, and discordant conditions together with their latencies which are in relation to the lamas and the Three Jewels. May all sentient beings, myself and others, enter under the refuge of the lamas and the Three Jewels.

Believe that all have entered under the refuge of the Three Jewels.

Then, to [generate] an aspiration to enlightenment for all sentient beings, say, 'By whatever merit I have done, my gifts and so forth, may I accomplish Buddhahood for the sake of all beings.'

Think at this time:

By the roots of virtue arising from giving, ethics, and meditation, which I perform, or I ask others to perform, or which are done by others with my sympathy, may I attain the state of completely perfect Buddhahood for the sake of all sentient beings. I *will* attain the state of completely perfect Buddhahood for the sake of all sentient beings. For the sake of achieving Buddhahood I will learn according to Buddha's way the [compassionate] deeds of the sons of the Conqueror Buddha. I pray for empowerment from the lamas and gods to enable me to do this.

Make the prayer with strong force. Thereby the gatherings of lamas and gods [visualized in space in front of you] are pleased; a duplicate separates from each of their bodies and dissolves into you. Thus, your body momentarily changes into the body of lama and Buddha. Rays of light emanate from your body transformed into lama and Buddha. By striking all the sentient beings living around you the rays of light purify their sins and obstructions. Think that they have been established in the state of lama and Buddha. This is said to be the extraordinary precept of the oral lineage of En-sa [dbEn-sa], meditation in which one actualizes while on the path the result of the generation of the aspiration to enlightenment.

Then, think:

What causes the wandering of all sentient beings, the old mothers, in cyclic existence without independence?

By the power of the two, desire and hatred [which are apprehensions of other beings as] intimate or alien, they wander in cyclic existence and thereby undergo suffering.

Therefore, if all sentient beings were to abide in the immeasurable equanimity which is free of desire and hatred, intimacy and alienness, how nice it would be! May they come to abide so. I will cause them to abide so. I pray for empowerment from the lamas and gods to enable me to do this.

If all sentient beings had happiness and the causes of happiness, how nice it would be! May they come to have these. I will cause them to have these. I pray for empowerment from the lamas and gods to enable me to do this.

If all sentient beings were free from suffering and the causes of suffering, how nice it would be! May they come to be free from these. I will cause them to be free from these. I pray for empowerment from the lamas and gods to enable me to do this.

If all sentient beings did not lack high status [as humans and gods] and the excellent bliss of liberation, how nice it would be! May they come not to lack these. I will cause them not to lack these. I pray for empowerment from the lamas and gods to enable me to do this.

Make the supplication with strong force and imagine the purification of all sentient beings through the falling ambrosia.

[The generation of the aspiration to enlightenment in general is the development of the thought:] 'I must attain, regardless of anything, the precious state of a completely perfect Buddha, quickly, quickly for the sake of all sentient beings, the mothers.' The generation of the attitude of altruistic enlightenment in particular [in this book is the development of the thought]: 'For the sake of attaining Buddhahood I will begin meditation on the instructions of the three principal aspects of the path.' Mentally promise firm adherence to this, and also say it many times.

Then, the objects of refuge [which are visualized in space in front of you] melt into light by stages from the outside [to the inside of the group] and dissolve into the master lama in the centre [Tsong-ka-pa]. The master lama also melts into light and dissolves into your forehead between the eyebrows. Consider this as empowerment for your mental continuum.

[The fourth of the six practices of preparation is] the clear setting of the field of assembly in visualization in front of you. There is the broad and extensive trunk of a wish-granting tree in the space directly in front of you. The top has leaves, flowers, and fruit. On its top of one hundred thousand petals eight great lions are supporting a high and broad throne of jewels. On that, on cushions of variegated lotus and sun and moon is your kind fundamental lama in actuality but in the form of the great Tsong-ka-pa, the King of Doctrine, with clear white body and mouth smiling with pleasure. He is wearing the three religious robes and the golden *paṇḍita*'s hat. His two hands are performing the gesture of the wheel of doctrine at his heart and hold stems of lotuses which extend over his shoulders.

On the blossoming lotus above his right shoulder the wisdom of all the Buddhas shines forth in the form of a sword. The light fills all worlds. All the collections of the darkness of ignorance [particularly the apprehension of inherently existing entities] are consumed by the fire burning forth from its point.

On the blossoming lotus above his left shoulder is a volume of the *Perfection of Wisdom* in one hundred thousand stanzas, the sole mother of all the Buddhas of the three times [past, present, and future]. Letters of melted gold shine from the sapphire pages; the emanation of rays of light from the letters clears away the darkness of sentient beings' ignorance. Also, the letters are not just shapes; they clearly proclaim the initial process of generating the aspiration to enlightenment through to finally effecting the welfare of migrators in cyclic existence through the twenty-seven activities of a Buddha—together with the grounds, paths, and fruits. Think that potentialities predisposing you to the Mahāyāna path can be established just by the sound's coming to the mind.

The Conqueror Śākyamuni Buddha is sitting in the heart of the master lama. The Conqueror Vajradhara is sitting in the heart of Śākyamuni Buddha. In each of the hair pores of the master lama's body there are numberless Buddha fields. Rays of light emanate from all parts of his body in the ten directions. At the points of these rays inconceivable magical creations, equal in number to sentient beings, emanate and perform actions for the sake of those migrators.

The master lama sits in the middle of the encirclement of a five-coloured rainbow with his legs crossed in the adamantine posture. On a ray of light which has emanated upward from his heart, the beings from the Conqueror Vajradhara through to the fundamental lama who actually bestowed this teaching on you sit one above the other. Not including the Conqueror Vajradhara, all from Mañjuśrī through to your own fundamental lama are each in actuality the lama himself in the form of an orange Mañjuśrī. His right hand holds aloft a sword; his left hand holds a volume at his heart. Meditate on these as having only the nature of light.

On the point of a ray of light emanating to the right from the heart of the master lama, the lamas of the lineage of the extensive [compassionate] deeds are sitting on cushions of lotus and moon. On the point of a ray of light emanating to the left from the heart of the master lama the lamas of the lineage of the deep view [that phenomena do not exist by way of their own being] are sitting on cushions of lotus and moon. On the point of a ray of light emanating to the front from the heart of the master lama the lamas who have actual doctrinal relationship to you are sitting on cushions of lotus and moon.

Surrounding the master lama, collections of deities, Buddhas, Bodhisattvas, Heroes, Sky-Goers, and Protectors of Doctrine are sitting on lion thrones. On marvellous tables in front of each of the members of the field of assembly are the verbal doctrines taught by each of them in the form of books having the nature of light. At the crown of the head of each of the members of the field of assembly appears a white *oṃ*; at the throat a red *āḥ*; at the heart a blue *hūṃ* [pronounced 'hoong']. Rays of light emanate in the ten directions from the *hūṃ* of the heart.

[You have been imagining beings of wisdom in the sky in front of you]. Now invite the actual beings of wisdom, who are like those imagined, from their usual places [such as Amitābha from Sukhāvatī]. All come and dissolve into each of the imagined beings. Thus, firmly consider each as an entity which includes all three refuges [Buddha, Doctrine, and Spiritual Community].

Then, generate [visualize, feel, and so forth] yourself as a deity, and offer ritual ablution, clothing, and so forth [to the beings of wisdom]. If these are done, it makes a great difference with respect to clarifying the mind for cultivating the path and for pacifying uncleanliness, defilements, and so forth. Yet, even if the ablution is not done, it is said there is no fault which would nullify [the practice].

Produce a bath-house:

In a bath-house of very pleasant fragrance,
With a base of crystal, clear and sparkling clean,
With attractive, flaming pillars of precious stone,
And covered with a canopy of shining pearls:

Offer ablution:

Just as the gods offered ablution
[To Buddha] just after his birth,
So with pure divine water
I also offer ablution.
Oṃ sarva tathāgata abhiṣekata samaya śrīye aḥ hūṃ.

I offer ablution to the King of Conquerors, Vajradhara,
Whose body is fashioned from tens of millions of perfect, good virtues,
Whose speech fulfils the hopes of limitless migrators,
Whose mind sees all objects of knowledge just as they are.
Oṃ sarva tathāgata abhiṣekata samaya śrīye aḥ hūṃ.

I offer ablution to the lineage of extensive deeds.
I offer ablution to the lineage of the profound view.
I offer ablution to the lineage empowering practice.
I offer ablution to the lineaged lamas.
Oṃ sarva tathāgata abhiṣekata samaya śrīye aḥ hūṃ.

I offer ablution to the teachers, the Buddhas.
I offer ablution to the protection, the Doctrine.
I offer ablution to the leaders, the Spiritual Community.
I offer ablution to the sources of refuge, the Three Jewels.
Oṃ sarva tathāgata abhiṣekata samaya śrīye aḥ hūṃ.

Wipe their bodies:

I wipe their bodies with a clean cloth, infused with fragrance, unequalled.
Oṃ hūṃ traṃ hrīḥ aḥ kāya viśodhanaye svāhā.

Anoint their bodies:

Just as a goldsmith polishes pure gold,
So I anoint the shining bodies of these Kings
Of Conquerors with the best of fragrances, strong perfumes
Suffusing all the billion [worlds of this world system].

Offer clothing:

With indestructible faith I offer
Fine, soft, light, divine clothing to those
Who have attained an indestructible adamantine body.
Thereby, may I attain an adamantine body.

Offer ornaments:

Because the Conquerors possess the natural ornaments of [a Buddha's] major and minor marks
They cannot be decorated with other ornaments; however,
Through my offering the best of precious ornaments may all migrators
Attain a body adorned with the major and minor marks.

Petition them to remain:

O Conquerors, because you love me and all migrators,
I petition you to remain here
Through your magical emanations
As long as I make offerings.

In order to pacify sins and infractions which are conditions opposed to cultivation of the path and in order to increase merits which are conditions concordant with cultivation of the path, perform the seven branches of practice together with offering *maṇḍalas* [the fifth practice of preparation]. These seven include the essentials of accumulation of merit and purification of obstructions.

Doing it in the long way, bow down and say whatever names of Buddhas, Bodhisattvas, and lineaged lamas you know. In the short form say:

I bow down respectfully to the spiritual guides,
The eyes that see all the countless scriptures,
The best fords for the fortunate progressing to liberation.
They clearly act through skill in means aroused by love.

1. OBEISANCE

I bow down with pure body, speech, and mind
To all without exception of all
The lions of men, the Tathāgatas of the three times
In the worlds of the ten directions.

Through the power of my aspirations for good deeds
I bow down to all the Conquerors with extreme respect,
Myself adopting forms as numerous as the particles of the worlds,
And with all the Conquerors vivid before my mind.

I consider that in one particle are Buddhas as numerous
As the particles of the worlds, sitting in the middle
Of Buddha Sons, and that the Conquerors fill all
Without exception of the entities of phenomena.

I praise all the Sugatas and express
The qualities of all the Conquerors with all
The oceans of sounds of the melodious intoner [the tongue],
Inexhaustible oceans praising them.

2. OFFERING

I offer to all the Conquerors
Excellent flowers, excellent garlands,
Pleasant sounds, fragrant ointments,
Superior umbrellas, superior lamps, and excellent incense.

I offer to all the Conquerors
Excellent clothing, superior fragrances,
Fragrant powders, and mounds of incense equal to Mount Meru,
And all specially arrayed marvels.

I also consider all extensive, unequalled acts
Of offering to be for all the Conquerors.
By the powers of faith in good deeds
I bow down and revere all the Conquerors.

Say that softly with visualization of the field of assembly and bow down.

At this interval confess each of the three vows [the vow of individual emancipation, the Bodhisattva vow, and the tantric vow] and in particular recite the *Confession of Infractions* and bow down as much as possible.

Say softly, with visualization of the field of assembly and of the falling ambrosia, the following prayer.

3. CONFESSION

I confess individually all sins
Done by me with body, speech,
Or mind through the power of
Desire, hatred, and ignorance.

4. ADMIRATION

I admire and will emulate the meritorious actions
Of all the Conqueror Buddhas of the ten directions,
The Buddha Sons, the Solitary Realizers, those still learning,
Those with no more learning, and all migrators.

5. ENTREATY

I entreat all the protectors, who have found non-attachment
And have progressively awakened into enlightenment
And are the lights of the world systems of the ten directions,
To turn the unsurpassed wheel [of doctrine].

6. SUPPLICATION

I supplicate with pressed palms those planning
To show *nirvāṇa* to the world to dwell here
Even as many aeons as the particles in the realms
To help and bring happiness to all migrators.

7. DEDICATION

I dedicate all the little virtue
I have accumulated through obeisance,
Offering, confession, admiration, entreaty,
And supplication toward perfect enlightenment.

Then, offer *maṇḍalas* extensively:

Oṃ vajra bhūmi āḥ hūṃ. Ground of most powerful gold. *Oṃ vajra rekhe āḥ hūṃ.* In the centre surrounded by an outer rim of iron mountains, the king of mountains, Meru. To the east, Videha with Deha and Videha. To the south, Jambudvīpa with Cāmara and Aparacāmara. To the west, Godānīya with Śāthā and Uttaramantriṇa. To the north, Kuru with Kurava and Kaurava. Mountains of jewels, wish-granting trees, wish-granting cows, naturally grown maize, precious chariots, precious jewels, precious consorts, precious ministers, precious elephants, precious horses, precious generals, vessels of great treasure, goddess of beauty, goddess of garlands, goddess of song, goddess of dance, goddess of flowers, goddess of incense, goddess of light, goddess of perfume, suns, moons, precious umbrellas, banners of victory, and in the centre all the marvellous wealth of gods and humans. I offer these to the glorious excellent lamas—the kind fundamental lamas and their lineages—and to the divine company of Tsong-ka-pa, the King of Subduers Śākyamuni Buddha, and Vajradhara together with their retinues. Please take these through your compassion for the sake of migrators. Having taken them, please empower me with blessings.

I offer this ground anointed with incense,
Strewn with flowers, adorned with Meru, the four continents,
Sun, and moon and visualized as a Buddha Land;
May all migrators enjoy this Pure Land.

To the lamas, deities, and Three Jewels I offer in visualization
The body, speech, mind, and resources of myself and others,
Our collections of virtue in the past, present, and future,
And the wonderful precious *maṇḍala* with the masses of Samantabhadra's offerings.
Accepting them through your compassion, please empower me with blessings.
Idaṃ guru ratna maṇḍalakaṃ niryātayāmi.

Making a petition, recite three times this prayer, *The Three Great Aims*, which was composed by the master lama [Tsong-ka-pa] himself:

I pray for empowerment to stop all the various wrong thoughts, beginning from not respecting the spiritual guide through to conceiving persons and phenomena to exist inherently. I pray for empowerment in order to generate easily all the various correct attitudes, from respecting the spiritual guide through to realizing the reality of selflessness. I pray for empowerment in order to pacify immediately all internal and external obstacles.

[The sixth preparatory practice is a supplication.] Make a supplication to the lineage of lamas who teach the principal aspects of the path, saying:

I supplicate the Conqueror Vajradhara, protector of mundane existence and solitary peace,
Who does not abide in the extremes of mundane existence and solitary peace,
Who through wisdom has ended the bonds of mundane existence,
And who through compassion has put far away the liking for a solitary peace.

I supplicate the protector Mañjuśrī, body of wisdom
Unifying all the treasures of wisdom
Of countless Buddhas exceeding even
A number equal to the particles of the realms.

I supplicate to the feet of Pa-po-dor-jay [dPa'-po-rdo-rje]
All of whose webs of doubt were manifestly cleared away
By the holy Mañjuśrī through the powers of his prayers
Like a great wave set rolling long ago.

I supplicate to the feet of the glorious lama Tsong-ka-pa
Who manifested the Three Buddha Bodies through his good logical realization
Of the way the two truths actually are and through
His practice of the union of method and wisdom.

I supplicate to the feet of the world's scholar, Gen-dun-drup [dGe-'dun-grub]

Lion expounding the good path, glittering with the mane
Of the hundred thousand books
In the forest of the Sugata's scriptures.

May I be empowered effortlessly to generate
Faith and respect at all times through only remembering
The kind masters, the basis of all qualities
Of auspicious virtue, mundane and supramundane.

May I be empowered to produce contentment of mind,
Few desires, abiding in discipline, heartily seeking liberation,
Speaking honestly, forever being conscientious, acquaintance with superior friends,
Perceiving everything as pure, and lack of bias.

May I be empowered to produce in my mental continuum
Untainted realization of the shortness of time and a profound aversion
For goods and respect through remembering not just the words
That death is definite and the time of death is indefinite.

May I be empowered effortlessly to generate
Compassion and a disinclination toward achieving only my own happiness
Through identifying all embodied beings as kind mothers
And thus becoming aware of the suffering of the stricken beings.

May I be empowered to understand in accordance
With the thoughts of the Superior, the 'father' Nāgārjuna, and his spiritual son [Āryadeva],
The deep meaning of dependent-arising free from extremes,
The sole medicine curing all the sickness of extreme conceptions.

Taking as an example the virtue of this prayer,
May all the roots of virtue of myself and others
In the past, present, and future not ripen for even a moment
As anything unfavourable to superior enlightenment:

Desire for profit, fame, companions,
Enjoyments, goods, and others' respect.
May all my roots of virtue become in birth after birth
Causes only of supreme enlightenment.

May the forms of these pure wishes be accomplished
Through the Conqueror's and his sons' marvellous empowerment,
Through the universal truth of dependent-arising,
And through my pure extraordinary thoughts.

Make these supplications with strong force in order to generate in your mental continuum quickly the realization of the three principal aspects of the path to highest enlightenment.

II. THE SESSION: DEVELOPING AN UNDERSTANDING OF THE PATH AND PROMISING TO CULTIVATE IT

Meditate continuously on the gatherings of lamas and gods visualized in space in front of you, and think:

In general, the foundation of all good qualities is faith. In particular, the foundation of all accumulations of goodness in this life and the future, the fundamental support of all achievements—superior and common—the excellent cause of producing, keeping, increasing, and completing all stages and paths is proper reliance on an excellent spiritual guide. Therefore, at the beginning I must experience reliance on a spiritual guide. Such reliance is the base of the path.

The ways of reliance on a spiritual guide are two: reliance in thought and reliance in deed. With respect to the first, how to rely on a spiritual guide in thought, clearly set [visualize] in the space in front of you the virtuous spiritual guides who teach doctrine to you, and firmly think:

These spiritual guides of mine are actually Buddhas. In the precious *tantras* the completely perfect Buddha says that the Conqueror Vajradhara in the degenerate era shows himself in the physical form of virtuous spiritual guides and performs deeds for the sake of migrators in cyclic existence. Just so, these virtuous spiritual guides of mine are only showing a form of body different [from Vajradhara's customary body]. Except for that, they are the Conqueror Vajradhara who in the degenerate era displays the physical form of virtuous spiritual guides in order to take care of those who did not have the fortune actually to see the Buddha.

These kind fundamental lamas of mine are not only in fact real Buddhas; their kindness is even greater than all the Buddhas'. If all the former Conquerors and their sons forsook me, unable to tame me, these kind fundamental lamas, not able to bear it because of their compassion, performed the deeds of the Conqueror. Even if Buddha actually came, he would teach deep doctrines which would not be better expressed.

In the past, our teacher, Buddha, the King of Conquerors, for the sake of only one stanza of doctrine even put a thousand iron nails into his body and used his body to burn a thousand lamps. Without regret he gave up his son, his wife, his own body, and all usable things, whatever he had. He had to do difficult deeds unencompassable by thought. Without my having to do any such difficult deeds, these kind fundamental lamas, like a father teaching his son, liberally teach me deep precepts, the Mahāyāna doctrines, complete and without mistake. If I can meditate on their teaching, it can easily give me the states of high status and even of liberation from cyclic existence as well as omniscience. There is no way at all to return such kindness.

Meditate thus until the hairs of the body rise and tears well from the eyes.

The ways of relying on a spiritual guide through deeds are to please him with the three delights. The three delights are to offer things to him, to venerate him with body and speech, and to achieve what he teaches. Of these three, the main one is to achieve what he teaches. Therefore, think:

According to the lama's teaching I must practise the meaning of all the scriptures together with their commentaries included in the three principal aspects of the path.

Mentally promise firm adherence to this.

How are all the meanings of the scriptures with their commentaries included in the three principal aspects of the path?

The chief content of all the scriptures with their commentaries is only the means of freeing trainees from bad migrations in particular and cyclic existence in general and of establishing them in the state of Buddhahood. In order to attain Buddhahood it is necessary to learn its two causes, method and wisdom. Further, the chief method is the aspiration to highest enlightenment for the sake of all sentients beings, and the chief wisdom is the correct view that no phenomenon exists by way of its own being.

In order to generate these two paths in your mental continuum it is necessary at the beginning to generate all the features of the thought that you will definitely leave cyclic existence. This thought is a wish for liberation from cyclic existence. If you do not want liberation from cyclic existence, you cannot generate the aspiration to enlightenment and love and compassion, which are wishes to free other sentient beings from cyclic existence.

The main means of attaining a Buddha's Form Body is the collection of merit. The heart, root, and excellent essential of all the collections of merit is just the precious aspiration to highest enlightenment. The main cause of attaining a Buddha's Wisdom Body, which is the mind of the Conqueror, is the collection of wisdom. The heart, root, and excellent essential of all the accumulations of wisdom is just the correct view that no phenomenon exists by way of its own being.

Therefore, all the essentials of the path are included in the three: the thought definitely to leave cyclic existence, the altruistic aspiration to highest enlightenment, and the correct view. The practice of these is the excellent pith of all quintessential instructions. In just this way the protector Mañjuśrī earnestly exhorted the great Tsong-ka-pa, King of Doctrine.

Thus, first of all, the root of all accumulations of goodness derives from reliance on a spiritual guide. Therefore, at the beginning it is necessary to have practical experience in relying on a spiritual guide.

The basic text, Tsong-ka-pa's *Three Principal Aspects of the Path to Highest Enlightenment*, says:

I bow down to the holy lamas.

This also [implicitly] indicates all the other surrounding practices of preparation just explained.

At the beginning of cultivating the path, you must gain a rough idea of the entire body of the path. Aim in thought, 'I must cultivate such a number and series of paths.' It is necessary to make a promise of firm adherence to a particular meditation and not to pass from it to other subjects. Tsong-ka-pa's basic text says:

I will explain as well as I can
The meaning of the essence of all the Conqueror's scriptures,
The path praised by the excellent Conqueror and sons,
And the port for the fortunate wishing liberation.
Whoever are not attached to the pleasures of mundane existence,
Whoever strive in order to make leisure and fortune worthwhile,
Whoever have faith in the path which pleases the Conqueror Buddha,
Those fortunate ones should listen with an undistracted mind.

III. THE ACTUAL MEDITATION:
1. HOW TO CULTIVATE A THOUGHT TO LEAVE CYCLIC EXISTENCE

Tsong-ka-pa's *Three Principal Aspects of the Path* says:

Without a complete thought definitely to leave
Cyclic existence there is no way to stop
Seeking pleasurable effects in the ocean of existence.
Also, craving cyclic existence thoroughly binds
The embodied; therefore, in the beginning a thought
Definitely to leave cyclic existence should be sought.

This section has two parts, how to meditate on the means to cease looking forward to the appearances of this life and how to meditate on the means to cease looking forward to the appearances of future lives.

THE MEANS TO CEASE LOOKING FORWARD TO THE APPEARANCES OF THIS LIFE

Tsong-ka-pa's *Three Principal Aspects of the Path* says:

Leisure and fortune are difficult to find
And life has no duration,
Through familiarity with this, emphasis on
The appearances of this life is reversed.

This section has two parts, thought on the meaningfulness of leisure and fortune and thought on the difficulty of finding leisure and fortune.[1]

The meaningfulness of leisure and fortune

Continuously meditate on the lamas and gods in front of you, and think:

Leisure means having the time to accomplish the excellent doctrine of Buddha. Fortune means having all the inner and outer conditions conducive to realizing the doctrine.

Therefore, this life of complete leisure and fortune which we have obtained is extremely worthwhile. Using such a life we can accomplish giving, ethics, patience, effort, and so forth, which are the causes of the wonderful body and resources of high status. In particular, in a life of leisure and fortune we can generate the three vows and can easily accomplish the state of perfect Buddhahood in one short lifetime during the degenerate era. This life of worthwhile leisure and fortune is difficult to find, and if it is found, its essence should be used without wasting it pointlessly. I pray for empowerment from the lamas and gods to enable me to do this.

The difficulty of finding leisure and fortune

Clearly visualize the gatherings of lamas and gods in front of you, and think:

This life of complete leisure and fortune not only is meaningful but also is extremely difficult to find. Most beings, including humans, for the most part engage in the ten non-virtuous actions, which are obstacles to obtaining leisure and fortune. In particular, in order to obtain all aspects of a life-support of complete leisure and fortune one needs a basis [of a complete action] of ethics [which establishes the main potency in the mind which, when empowered, produces a human life]. One needs helping causes, giving and so forth [which establish potencies that supplement the main potency]. One also needs conjunction of one life to another by means of a stainless vow [to gain enlightenment for the sake of others].

Those who muster such causes are extremely few. Those in bad migrations—animals, hungry ghosts, and hell-beings—seem to be beyond hope of obtaining even a happy migration. Also, the obtaining of a life-support of complete leisure and fortune by those in happy migrations [humans and gods of the desire realm] is as rare as a star at noon. Therefore, the essence of this life of complete leisure and fortune, difficult to find and meaningful when found, must be used without wasting it pointlessly.

This is how to use the essence of this life of leisure and fortune:

I will continuously rely on the lama inseparable from Buddha, and I will practise the essentials of the Mahāyāna precepts taught by him. Thereby, I will attain perfect Buddhahood in only one lifetime. I pray for empowerment from the lamas and gods to enable me to do this.

THE MEANS TO CEASE LOOKING FORWARD TO THE APPEARANCES OF FUTURE LIVES

Tsong-ka-pa's *Three Principal Aspects of the Path* says:

If you think again and again
About deeds and their inevitable effects
And the sufferings of cyclic existence,
The emphasis on the appearances
Of future lives will be reversed.

This section has two parts, thought about deeds and their inevitable effects and thought on the sufferings of cyclic existence.

Deeds and their effects

Clearly visualize the collection of lamas and gods in front of you, and think:

It is said in the scriptures of the Conqueror Buddha, 'From causes which are virtuous deeds only effects of happiness arise; suffering does not arise. From causes which are non-virtuous deeds only effects of suffering arise. Though one creates even tiny causes—virtues and sins—extremely great effects—happiness and suffering—arise. If virtuous and sinful deeds are not done, one does not experience effects of happiness and suffering. If interference with virtuous and sinful causes already made is not encountered, the deeds done will not be fruitless; effects—happiness and suffering—will certainly come forth.'

I will generate firm faith trusting what was taught with regard to the greater power of deeds from the point of view of the field of activity, the thought, the object, and the agent. Then I will learn the right way to adopt virtues and discard non-virtues. Among the ten virtues I will as much as possible achieve even tiny virtues and among the ten non-virtues will not pollute the three doors of body, speech, and mind with even tiny non-virtues. I pray for empowerment from the lamas and gods to enable me to do this.

The sufferings of cyclic existence

This section has two parts, thought on the sufferings of cyclic existence in general and thought on the sufferings of individual cyclic existences.

Of cyclic existence in general

Clearly visualize the gatherings of lamas and gods in front of you, and think:

Once one has taken birth in cyclic existence due to [former polluted] deeds and the afflictions [of desire, hatred, and ignorance], one does not pass beyond suffering.

Because enemies become friends and friends become enemies, there is no certainty about someone's helping or harming.

However much the happiness of cyclic existence is enjoyed, not only is there no final satisfaction, but also attachments are extended, attracting many unbearable sufferings.

However good a body one obtains, as it must be given up again and again, there is no certainty with regard to obtaining a certain type of body.

Because the gap between lives is closed again and again beginninglessly, the limits of birth are not to be seen.

No matter what prosperity of cyclic existence is obtained, because finally if must definitely be forsaken, there is no certainty with regard to obtaining prosperity.

Because one must go alone to the next life, there is no certainty with regard to friends. Thus, at this time of obtaining a life of complete leisure and fortune which is difficult to find and, if found, is extremely worthwhile, I will do whatever I can to attain the state of lama and Buddha who have abandoned all the sufferings of cyclic existence. I pray for empowerment from the lamas and gods to enable me to do this.

Of individual cyclic existences

Clearly visualize the gatherings of lamas and gods in front of you, and think:

Once one has the contaminated aggregates of body and mind, one does not pass beyond suffering. Thus, what need is there to consider whether the three bad migrations—animals, hungry ghosts, and hell-beings—involve suffering!

Based on the contaminated aggregates of a human, one experiences hunger, thirst, hot, cold, and so forth. One experiences separation from attractive friends, meeting unattractive enemies, searching for but not finding the desired, the undesired falling upon oneself, birth, ageing, sickness, death, and so on.

Based on the contaminated aggregates of demi-gods, one experiences mental suffering from an unbearable jealousy of the glorious fortune of gods, and one experiences physical suffering [from consequently engaging in war].

Based on the contaminated aggregates of the desire gods, when there is fighting with the demi-gods, one experiences the cutting off of limbs, the loss of the body, murder, and so forth. There is also the undesirable foreknowledge from the arising of the signs of death that one must separate from the glorious fortune of gods and must experience the terrible suffering of a bad migration.

Based even on the contaminated aggregates of the form and formless realms, one experiences the measureless suffering of falling to a bad migration upon the exhaustion of the impetus of the former good actions [which caused the birth in the upper realm]. For, freedom to remain in those realms was not attained.

In short, once these contaminated aggregates exist, they act as the base of birth, ageing, sickness, death, and so forth in this life. The suffering of pain and the suffering of change are attracted to both this and future lives. In short, just the existence of the contaminated aggregates means that they are entities compounded from a force other than their own—former [polluted] actions and afflictions.

Therefore, I will do whatever I can to attain the state of lama and Buddha that frees one from the suffering of cyclic existence which has the nature of contaminated aggregates. I pray for empowerment from the lamas and gods to enable me to do this.

Dwell thus on the thoughts about cyclic existence in general and about particular cyclic existences without desirous attachment for any of the prosperity of cyclic existence—like the nausea of a prisoner for the prison. A strong intention to seek liberation all day and night will be generated. When this happens, it is taken as an indication that the thought that one will definitely leave cyclic existence has been generated.

Tsong-ka-pa's *Three Principal Aspects of the Path* says:

If, having meditated thus, you do not generate
Admiration even for an instant for the prosperity
Of cyclic existence and if an attitude
Seeking liberation arises day and night,
Then the thought definitely to leave
Cyclic existence has been generated.

Also, if this thought definitely to leave
Cyclic existence is not conjoined
With generation of a complete aspiration to highest enlightenment,
It does not become a cause of the marvellous
Bliss of unsurpassed enlightenment. Thus,
The intelligent should generate the supreme
Altruistic aspiration to enlightenment.

IV. THE ACTUAL MEDITATION: 2. HOW TO CULTIVATE AN ALTRUISTIC ASPIRATION TO HIGHEST ENLIGHTENMENT

The cultivation of an aspiration to highest enlightenment begins with the recognition of all sentient beings as mothers. This is done having first attained even-mindedness towards all sentient beings.

HOW TO ACHIEVE EVEN-MINDEDNESS

First, clearly imagine in front of you a neutral sentient being who has neither helped nor harmed you. Then think:

All persons want happiness and do not want suffering; thus, I must not help some apprehending them as intimate and must not harm others apprehending them as alien. I must create an even-mindedness that is free of desire and hatred, intimacy and alienness, with regard to all sentient beings. I pray for empowerment from the lamas and gods to enable me to do this.

When you become even-minded toward a neutral being, clearly imagine in front of you a sentient being who is definitely pleasant to the mind. Then cultivate an even-mindedness [which is devoid of desire and hatred]. Not becoming even-minded is due to the power of desire. Think that you have been born in beginningless cyclic existence by desiring the pleasant in the past and thereby stop attachment, and meditate.

When you become even-minded toward a pleasant being, clearly imagine in front of you a sentient being whom you know is definitely unpleasant. Then, cultivate even-mindedness [free of desire and hatred]. Not becoming even-minded is due to the generation of anger through single-mindedly apprehending the person to be disagreeable. If you do not become even-minded with regard to him, think that this is not the situation for generating an altruistic aspiration to enlightenment and thus stop anger, and meditate.

When you become even-minded toward an unattractive being, clearly imagine in front of you both a sentient being very pleasant, such as your mother, and a sentient being very unpleasant, such as an enemy. Then think:

These two are the same because from their point of view they want happiness and do not want suffering. From my point of view this one who is now apprehended as a friend has been my chief enemy countless times through beginningless cyclic existences. This one who is now apprehended as an enemy has been my mother limitless times through beginningless cyclic existences. Thus who should be desired? Who should be hated? I will create an even-mindedness which is free of desire and hatred, intimacy and alienness. I pray for empowerment from the lamas and gods to enable me to do this.

When you become even-minded toward an attractive being and an unattractive being together, cultivate an even-mindedness toward all sentient beings. The way to do this is to think:

All sentient beings are the same. From their point of view they want happiness and do not want suffering. Also, from my point of view all sentient beings are friends. Therefore, I will create an even-mindedness which is free of desire and hatred, intimacy and alienness, toward all of them. I will not help some because of apprehending them as intimate and will not harm others because of apprehending them as alien. I pray for empowerment from the lamas and gods to enable me to do this.

HOW TO CULTIVATE RECOGNITION OF ALL SENTIENT BEINGS AS MOTHERS

After that, there is the meditation which starts from recognition of all sentient beings as mothers and goes through to the altruistic aspiration to highest enlightenment. Continuously meditate on the lamas and gods in front of you, and think:

Why are all sentient beings my friends? Cyclic existence is beginningless; therefore, my births are also beginningless. In the continuum from one birth to another there is not even one country or place where I was not born. My births there are countless. There is not even one type of body of a sentient being that I did not formerly have. The times I had such bodies are countless. There is not even one sentient being who has not been my mother. The times each was my mother are countless. There is not even one sentient being who has not been my mother in a human body. The times each has been my mother are countless, and each will be my mother again in the future. Therefore, of course, they are my mothers who protected me with kindness.

HOW TO CULTIVATE A THOUGHT OF THE KINDNESS OF MOTHERS

If experience arises with regard to recognizing all sentient beings as mothers, think of their kindness. Continuously meditate on the lamas and gods in front of you, and visualize the clear form of your own mother of this life, not in her youth but in her old age. Then think:

This mother of mine was my mother not only in this life but also countless times again and again in the beginningless continuum of lives. In particular, in this life she initially protected me with love in the womb. Then when I was born, she placed me on a soft cushion; she rocked me to and fro on the tips of her ten fingers. She held me to the warmth of her flesh; she pleased me with her loving smile; she looked at me with happy eyes. She cleaned away the mucus in my nose with her mouth; she wiped away my filth with her hand.

My mother suffered more from my being slightly sick than she would have, for instance, if she herself were dying. She lovingly gave me food and riches which she obtained with strained muscles, without looking to her own life and without caring about sins, sufferings, and all the bad talk of others which she might incur. My mother provided measureless help and happiness for me in accordance with her condition. She protected me from measureless harm and suffering; therefore, her kindness is extremely great.

When experience arises with respect to the mother's kindness, meditate also on the kindness of other relatives and friends, such as your father. Clearly imagine the form of your father and so forth and think:

In the beginningless continuum of lives he was my mother innumerable times. He protected me with kindness when he was my mother just as my mother of this lifetime protected me with kindness. Therefore, his kindness is extremely great.

When experience arises with respect to the kindness of all relatives, meditate on all the neutral sentient beings. Clearly imagine them in front of you. Think:

It indeed appears that now these have no connection with me, but they have been my mother innumerable times in the beginningless continuum of lives. When they were my mother, they protected me with kindness just as my mother of this life protected me. Thus, their kindness is extremely great.

When experience arises with respect to the kindness of all neutral beings, meditate on sentient beings who are enemies and the like. Clearly imagine in front of you the forms of enemies, and think:

What is accomplished by apprehending these as enemies? They have been my mother countless times in the beginningless continuum of lives. When they were my mother, they provided measureless help and happiness for me. They protected me from measureless harm and suffering. In particular, I could not live even a little while without them [because I loved them so much]. They also could not live even a little while without me [because they loved me so much]. Thus, they had such an intimate sentiment toward me numberless times. That they have become enemies at the present occasion is due to bad actions; otherwise, they are only my mothers who protected me with kindness.

When experience arises with respect to the kindness of enemies, contemplate the kindness of all sentient beings.

HOW TO MEDITATE ON REPAYING THEIR KINDNESS

After thinking of their kindness as before, meditate on repaying their kindness. Continuously meditate on the lamas and gods in front of you, and think:

The mothers who have beginninglessly protected me with kindness are mentally agitated through being possessed by the afflictions of desire, hatred, and ignorance. Due to not having attained independence of mind, they are crazed. They lack the eye that sees the paths of high status and definite goodness. They have no virtuous spiritual guide, no leader of the blind. They stumble each moment by the punishment of bad deeds, passing along the edge of the abyss of frightful cyclic existences in general and bad migrations in particular. If I forsook them, I would be extremely shameless. Therefore, to repay their kindness I will free them from the sufferings of cyclic existence and will establish them in the bliss of liberation. I pray for empowerment from the lamas and gods to enable me to do this.

HOW TO CULTIVATE LOVE

Imagine an intimate such as your mother, and think:

How can she have bliss non-polluted [with thoughts of an inherently existing self]? She does not even have happiness polluted [with thoughts of an inherently existing self]. She goes along with what is now claimed to be happiness, which turns into suffering. Through wishing for happiness she strives, strives, yearns, yearns; however, she is making the causes of bad migrations and sufferings in the future. In this life, also, except for making suffering, fatigued and tired, she does not in the least have real bliss. Therefore, if she had happiness and all the causes of happiness, how nice it would be! May she come to have these. I will cause her to have these. I pray for empowerment from the lamas and gods to enable me to do this.

When experience arises with respect to the thought of love, imagine other relatives and friends such as your father. Then imagine neutral sentient beings, then enemies, and finally all sentient beings. Meditate as before.

HOW TO CULTIVATE GREAT COMPASSION AND THE UNUSUAL ATTITUDE

Think:

The kind fathers and mothers, throughout all of space, are bound without independence by polluted actions and afflictions. They are swept along powerlessly in the river of continuous cyclic existence by the currents of desire, existence [desire in the form and formless realms], ignorance, and wrong views. They are battered by the turbulent waves of birth, ageing, sickness, and death.

Their modes of action through body, speech, and mind are completely and tightly bound by the tight bonds of various actions difficult to oppose. They have entered beginninglessly into the iron cage of apprehending an inherently existent self and its belongings, which stays in the centre of the heart and is difficult for anyone to open. Thus, what is there to say about their being on the path going to liberation and omniscience? Without seeking even the path going to temporary happy migrations, the huge, thick, black cloud of ignorance that obscures the adopting of the good and the discarding of the bad has beclouded them. If I do not liberate these stricken beings tortured ceaselessly by the three sufferings—the suffering of pain, the suffering of change, and the pervasive suffering of being so conditioned as to be ready always to suffer pain—who will liberate them? If I were to abandon such stricken beings, the kind mothers, seeing them drowning in the ocean of cyclic existence, I would be shamelessly vulgar. I would be ashamed before the eyes of all the Buddhas and Bodhisattvas, and my wish to learn the Mahāyāna would also be only words. Therefore, now I will do whatever I can to generate an ability to free these stricken beings, the kind mothers, from cyclic existence and establish them in the state of Buddhahood.

Thus a complete form of a compassionate attitude that is unusual [in that you have taken upon yourself the burden of liberating all beings] should be generated with strong force.

HOW TO CULTIVATE AN ALTRUISTIC ASPIRATION TO HIGHEST ENLIGHTENMENT

Think:

Do I have the ability to establish all sentient beings in the state of Buddhahood?

If now I am unsure of where I am going, I have no ability to establish even one sentient being, myself, in the state of perfect Buddhahood. Also, even if I attain the state of a [Hearer or Solitary Realizer]

Foe Destroyer, aside from furthering a tiny bit the aims of sentient beings I will have no ability to establish all sentient beings in the state of Buddhahood. Who has such power? A completely perfect Buddha has. Therefore, I will do whatever I can to attain the state of a completely perfect, unsurpassed Buddha for the sake of all sentient beings, the mothers. I pray for empowerment from the lamas and gods to enable me to do this.

After generating an aspiration to highest enlightenment you should learn the activities of Bodhisattvas. Though the Bodhisattva activities involve limitless forms of practice, in brief they mean that within the context of being motivated by a precious aspiration to enlightenment for the sake of all sentient beings, you generate deep, penetrating ascertainment of the nature of the two truths in reliance on correct reasoning.

If experience arises through the turning of the mind to each of the six perfections and if the power of intellect proceeds to increase, perform all six perfections—giving, ethics, patience, effort, concentration, and wisdom—in each perfection. All the meanings of the Mahāyāna scriptures and the commentaries are included in the six perfections. Learn that all the activities of the Bodhisattvas do not pass beyond the six perfections.

Also, the four ways of gathering students are included in the six perfections. 'The gathering of students by giving gifts' is easy to understand [as being included in the perfection of giving]. 'Speaking pleasantly' is included in the giving of doctrine which is a part of giving. From among the three types of ethics—the ethics of vows, the ethics which are the composite of virtuous practices, and the ethics of aiding the aims of sentient beings—'teaching others to fulfil their aims' and 'one's acting according to this teaching' are included in the ethics of aiding the aims of sentient beings. [The main aims of sentient beings are the attainment of high status as humans and gods, liberation from cyclic existence, and Buddhahood.]

On the other hand, the four ways of gathering students can be presented separately from the perfections, for Bodhisattvas first learn to control their own mental continuum, and once having ripened that continuum they aid the aims of others. Therefore, in order to teach that it is necessary [to perform the perfections first and gather students later] the four ways of gathering students are often taught separately from the six perfections.

In short, say:

I will do whatever I can to attain the precious state of a completely perfect Buddha quickly, quickly for the sake of all sentient beings. In order to do that, I will generate an aspiration to highest enlightenment and will learn according to Buddha's way the exhortations [about the altruistic aspiration to highest enlightenment]. Then I will generate an aspiration to highest enlightenment in conjunction with the Bodhisattva deeds and will learn according to the way all the Bodhisattva deeds which are included in the six perfections and the four ways of gathering students. I pray for empowerment from the lamas and gods to enable me to learn these.

Make the petition with strong force.

You should experience as much as you can in the actual session a turning of the mind toward the altruistic aspiration to highest enlightenment and its exhortations. Between sessions also, you should learn to conjoin all activities of the three modes [of action, physical, verbal, and mental] with an aspiration to highest enlightenment for the sake of all sentient beings. Again and again you should clearly establish love, mercy, and the aspiration to highest enlightenment as the basis of all ways of behaviour. Even though only a fabricated aspiration to enlightenment is produced [rather than a spontaneous and effortless one], if whatever deeds done are conjoined with this aspiration they will become a means of finishing the collection of merit.

In the past King Prasenajit asked Buddha, the Blessed One, 'With too many activities, I am unable to remain single-mindedly in the practice of virtues. I wish to be able to practise the Mahāyāna without the degeneration of my activities as king. How can I do this?'

Buddha answered, 'Kings are unable to remain at all times single-minded with regard to the practice of virtues because they have many activities. They should cultivate this aspiration to enlightenment for the sake of all beings in relation to all ways of behaviour. They should be motivated in whatever they do by this aspiration. If they do this, everything they do will become a means of obtaining Buddhahood without neglecting the royal duties.' Because this is extremely important, that Bodhisattvas should learn to accompany everything they do with the aspiration to enlightenment was urgently taught also in [Śāntideva's] *Compendium of Instructions* (*Śikṣā-samuccaya*) quoting as the source this passage from the *Advice to King Prasenajit Sūtra.*

Moreover, when physical pain and mental suffering arise, meditate on giving pleasure to others and taking pain to yourself. Think:

> May the physical sickness and the mental suffering of all sentient beings throughout all of space leave them and be added to my physical sickness and mental suffering.

If happiness and the wonderful particulars of prosperity come to your body and mind, meditate on giving and taking. Think:

> I will give this happiness and fortune to all sentient beings [and take their unhappiness and misfortune].

When eating food, think:

> I will eat this food to nourish my body for the sake of all sentient beings. In addition, it is said that there are eighty-four thousand germs in my body, and by giving this food to them I attract them now with things; in the future I will attract them by giving them doctrine.

Generate such thought, and without wasting activities pointlessly, conjoin whatever you eat, drink, or do with generation of an altruistic aspiration to highest enlightenment. Even when lying down, you should go to sleep within an aspiration to enlightenment. Think:

> I will nourish my body with sleep for the sake of all sentient beings. I will nourish and further with sleep the various creatures in my body which sleep replenishes.

When cleaning the house, generate the thought:

> I will clean away the mess of actions and afflictions of all sentient beings.

At the time of bathing, cleaning your hands and so forth, generate the thought:

I will wash away the defilement of afflictions in all sentient beings.

When opening a door, generate the thought:

I will open the door of liberation to lead all sentient beings out of bad migrations and to lead them to the stage of Buddhahood.

When offering lamps to an image, generate the thought:

I will clear away the darkness of ignorance in all sentient beings throughout all of space.

Learn from these examples to conjoin all actions of the three modes [physical, verbal, and mental] with an aspiration to enlightenment. Learn from the mouth of an excellent lineaged lama and read in detail the Mahāyāna scriptures because the exhortations on the aspiration to enlightenment are as extensive and limitless as space.

About the ways of cultivating the generation of an altruistic aspiration to highest enlightenment Tsong-ka-pa's *Three Principal Aspects of the Path* says:

Also, if this thought definitely to leave
Cyclic existence is not conjoined
With generation of a complete aspiration to highest enlightenment,
It does not become a cause of the marvellous
Bliss of unsurpassed enlightenment. Thus,
The intelligent should generate the supreme
Altruistic aspiration to enlightenment.

[All ordinary beings] are carried
By the continuum of the four powerful currents,
Are tied with the tight bonds
Of actions difficult to oppose,
Have entered into the iron cage
Of apprehending an [inherently existent] self,
Are completely beclouded with the thick darkness of ignorance,
Are born into cyclic existence limitlessly,
And in their births are tortured

Ceaselessly by the three sufferings.
Thinking thus of the condition of mothers
Who have come to such a state,
Generate the supreme altruistic aspiration.

This is the system of practice as it appears in the quintessential instructions of the oral lineage.

V. THE ACTUAL MEDITATION: 3. HOW TO CULTIVATE A CORRECT VIEW

This section has two parts, meditation ascertaining the personal selflessness and meditation ascertaining the selflessness of other phenomena.

HOW TO MEDITATE SO AS TO ASCERTAIN PERSONAL SELFLESSNESS

Endless forms of reasoning for the ascertainment of selflessness were taught in the scriptures of the Conqueror Buddha. However, if it is ascertained through the four essentials of beginners, it is easy for it to become clear.

First essential: ascertaining the mode of appearance of what is negated in the theory of selflessness

Even in deep sleep we hold tightly, tightly, in the centre of the heart, the thought 'I, I'. This is the inborn misconception of a self. For example, without your having done a bad deed another accuses: 'You did such and such a bad deed', and you reflect tightly, tightly in the centre of the heart thinking 'I, I': 'Without my doing such a bad deed he accuses me like this.' At that time the way the 'I' is apprehended by the inborn misconception of a self is clearly manifest.

Therefore, at that time how and as what the mind apprehends the self should be analysed with a subtle part of the mind. If the later analytical attention is too strong, the former consciousness that conceives 'I, I' will be abandoned and will not appear at all [and thus cannot be watched]. Hence, allow the general mind to generate firmly and continuously the entity of that consciousness which thinks 'I', and analyse it with another subtle portion of consciousness.

When you analyse in this way, the first essential is to understand how the 'I' is conceived by the inborn conception of an inherently existent self:

This 'I' is not other than my own five aggregates or body and mind. The 'I' is not any of the five aggregates taken singly nor is it either of the two, body and mind, taken singly. Also, the 'I' is not just conceptually imputed to only the glittering collection of the five aggregates or a collection of the two, body and mind. Therefore, there is an 'I' which from the beginning is self-sufficient.

This deluded conception of an 'I' which from the start is self-sufficient is the inborn apprehension of an inherently existent 'I'. The 'I' that is its object is what is negated [in the theory of selflessness].

This way of identifying what is negated should be realized nakedly in your mental continuum without being just an idea explained by others or a general image produced by words. This is the first essential, ascertaining the mode of appearance of what is negated [in the theory of selflessness, a self-sufficient 'I'].

Second essential: ascertaining invariable concomitance

Since this 'I', which is conceived by a mind thinking 'I' tightly, tightly in the centre of the heart, exists in relation with your five aggregates, this 'I' is invariably either one with or different from the five aggregates. There is not at all a third way of their existing other than these two ways of existing. Phenomena must invariably exist in the form of one of these. Think and decide that there is not at all a third category of the existence of phenomena other than these two ways of existing.

Third essential: ascertaining the absence of true sameness

If it is thought that the 'I' is the same as the five aggregates, then just as one person has five aggregates, the 'I' would also be five continuums. Or in another way, just as the 'I' is one, the five aggregates would become a partless one. There are many such fallacies. Therefore, think that such an 'I' [a self-sufficient 'I'] is not one with the five aggregates.

Fourth essential: ascertaining the absence of true difference

Such an 'I' is not one with the five aggregates; however, you might think that it is different from the five aggregates.

After eliminating each of the aggregates, forms and so forth, the aggregate of consciousness can be identified separately, 'This is the aggregate of consciousness.' Just so, after eliminating each of the aggregates, the 'I' should be identified separately, 'This is the "I".' However, it is not so. Therefore, think that such an 'I' does not exist separately from the five aggregates.

Dwell thus on the analysis of the four essentials and determine that the 'I' as conceived by the inborn sense of an inherently existent self is non-existent. The continuum of this conviction should be sustained single-mindedly, without lethargy and without excitement. Moreover, if this conviction becomes weaker in strength, beginners, relying on having analysed the four essentials as above, should develop again a conviction of the unreality [of an 'I' which naturally exists and is not just imputed by thought]. Those of higher intelligence [have nakedly ascertained the way the self-sufficient 'I' actually does appear]. Relying on having analysed whether the 'I' as it is perceived by the inborn apprehender of 'I' exists or not, they should develop a conviction of the unreality [of a naturally existent 'I'] similar to the analysis of the four essentials.

At that time you should sustain single-mindedly the following two facets of understanding emptiness. From the point of view of ascertainment, firm definite knowledge determines that the 'I' does not inherently exist. Second, from the point of view of appearance there is an utter, clear vacuity which is only the absence of what is negated, that is, the true existence of 'I'. Sustaining these two single-mindedly is how to sustain the spacelike meditative equipoise.

Subsequent to meditative equipoise all phenomena, the 'I' and so forth, should be meditated on as the sport [of emptiness] like a magician's illusions. In other words, rely on developing a strong conviction of truthlessness [the knowledge that phenomena do not inherently exist] during meditative equipoise. Also afterwards learn to view all that appears, even though appearing [to exist inherently], as the sport [of emptiness] like a magician's illusions, truthless and false.

HOW TO MEDITATE SO AS TO ASCERTAIN THE SELFLESSNESS OF OTHER PHENOMENA

This section has two parts, meditation ascertaining that products do not inherently exist and meditation ascertaining that non-products do not inherently exist.

To ascertain the absence of inherent existence of products

Take the body as an example of a product. It undeniably appears to us [who do not know that phenomena do not inherently exist] that the body is a whole, looming body, self-sufficient, and is not just imputed by thought to this body which is only a collection of five limbs of bubbly flesh and bone. This is the mode of appearance of what is negated [in the theory of selflessness].

If such a whole body exists in relation with this body which is only a collection of five limbs of bubbly flesh and bone, it is one with or different from this body which is only a collection of five limbs of bubbly flesh and bone.

If they are one, then because this body which is only a collection of five limbs of bubbly flesh and bone is produced from the semen and blood of the father and mother, the drop of semen and blood that is the foundation of the entrance of consciousness would [absurdly] become the body which is only a collection of five limbs of bubbly flesh and bone. Also, just as there are five limbs, the body would become five bodies that are collections of five limbs.

[Then you might think that such a whole body] is different [from this body which is only a collection of five limbs of bubbly flesh and bone. In that case] after eliminating each of the limbs, head and so forth, [the identification] 'This is it', should be shown with respect to the body, but it is not possible. Therefore, develop conviction knowing that such an inherently existent body is totally non-existent, and sustain the realization single-mindedly.

To ascertain the absence of inherent existence of non-products

Take space as an example. There are many parts to space—directions and intermediate directions; analyse whether space exists as one with or different from these. Meditate as before and develop definite conviction in the unreality [of a naturally existent space].

In short, sustain well the two yogas. The first is the yoga of spacelike meditative equipoise. In it one sustains single-mindedly the conviction that there is not even a particle of any of the phenomena of cyclic existence and *nirvāṇa*, such as 'I', aggregate, mountain, fence, and house, that exists in its own right and is not just imputed by thought. The second is the yoga of illusion, the subsequent realization which [after the yoga of meditative equipoise] knows all objects of perception to be false entities that have the unreality of having arisen dependent upon a collection of major and minor causes. This meditative equipoise, which depends on sustaining the two yogas, is conjoined with a bliss of mental and physical pliancy that is induced by the power of analysis. It is assigned as actual special insight (*vipaśyanā*).

About cultivating a correct view, Tsong-ka-pa's *Three Principal Aspects of the Path* says:

If you do not have the wisdom
Realizing the way things are,
Even though you have developed the thought
Definitely to leave cyclic existence and
The altruistic aspiration to highest enlightenment,
The root of cyclic existence cannot be cut.
Therefore make effort at the means
Of realizing dependent-arising.

Whoever, seeing the cause and effect
Of all phenomena of cyclic existence and nirvāṇa
As inevitable, thoroughly destroys
The misapprehension of these objects
[As inherently existent] has entered
On a path pleasing Buddha.

As long as the two, realization of appearances, or
The inevitability of dependent-arising,
And realization of emptiness, or
The non-assertion [of inherent existence],
Appear to be separate,
There is still no realization
Of the thought of Śākyamuni Buddha.

When [the two realizations exist]
Simultaneously without alternation
And when, from only seeing dependent-arising
As universal, definite knowledge destroys
All the objects of the conception
[Of inherent existence], then the analysis
Of the view [of emptiness] is complete.

Further, the extreme of [inherent existence]
Is excluded [by knowledge of the nature]
Of appearances [existing only as worldly designations],
And the extreme of [total] non-existence
Is excluded [by knowledge of the nature]
Of emptiness [as the absence of inherent existence
And not the absence of nominal existence].

If within emptiness [of inherent existence]
The ways of the appearance of cause
And effect are known, you will not
Be captivated by extreme views.

The meaning of Tsong-ka-pa's words conveys the mode of practice as it appears in the precepts of the oral lineage.

VI. THE END OF THE SESSION

In the actual session you have developed as much as possible experience in transforming the mind through analytical meditation and stabilizing meditation. To conclude the session say many times:

I bow down, worship, and go for refuge to the feet of the lama undifferentiable from Mañjuśrī.

Think that by strongly making the prayer to the gatherings of lamas and gods all the members of the field of assembly melt into light by degrees from the limits and dissolve into Mañjuśrī and the master lama [Tsong-ka-pa who is one with Mañjuśrī]. Mañjuśrī together with the master lama dissolve into you. Thus all physical impurities—sickness and so forth—and all mental sins and obstructions are purified, and you suddenly appear in the body of Mañjuśrī.

Your own body has been radiantly transformed into the body of Mañjuśrī, and the emanation of rays of light from it, by striking all the sentient beings throughout all of space, establishes all sentient beings in the state of Mañjuśrī. Also, consider that the impurities of all inanimate objects are purified and that all inanimate things become as marvellous mansions [having the nature of light]. Contemplate as much as possible the billions of purified inanimate things and animate beings. Then establish a series of *mantra* in the heart of yourself and all sentient beings radiantly transformed into Mañjuśrī, reciting as much as you can, '*Oṃ a ra pa tsa na di*' [three, seven, twenty-one, etc., times; the last time repeat *di di di di di di* . . . as many times as possible].

At the end say:

After I have quickly attained
Through the virtue of this session
The state of Mañjuśrī, may I establish
All migrators in his state.

I dedicate and consider the very wholesome virtue
Done in this session as the cause of accomplishing
All the prayers of all the Sugatas
And their sons of the past, present, and future,
And as the cause of [the world's] maintaining
The excellent doctrine, verbal and cognitive.

Through the power of this virtue
May I finish travelling the path
Of the thought definitely to leave cyclic existence,
The altruistic aspiration to highest enlightenment,
The correct view, and the two stages of *tantra*
In all my continuum of lives, never losing the four wheels of the Mahāyāna.

I will follow like a son after his father, making sincere effort to achieve the three principal aspects of the path which include the essentials of all the scriptures.

The basic text, Tsong-ka-pa's *Three Principal Aspects of the Path* says:

When you have realized thus just as they are
The essentials of the three principal aspects of the path,
Resort to solitude and generate the power of effort.
Accomplish quickly your final aim, my son.

Thus the lama Mañjunātha [Tsong-ka-pa] advised us followers with compassion.

If your mind becomes well practised with respect to the path of the common vehicle, you should enter the immutable vehicle, the *Vajrayāna*, the unsurpassed quick path of purification in one short lifetime of the degenerate era without taking three countless aeons. Also, you should please with the three delights a tantric guru who has all the attributes, and your mental continuum will be ripened through the pure powers of initiation.

Maintain dearer than your life the protection of promises and vows accepted at the time of initiation. Based on that, search well for the essentials of the two stages of the profound path, the essential meaning of the ocean of *tantras*. If unmistaken ascertainment of the meaning is found, apply yourself to yoga in four sessions. There is no greater practice than learning thus the entire body of the paths of both *sūtra* and *tantra*. This is the ultimate pith of quintessential instructions extracting the essence of lama Mañjunātha's mind.

It was said from the mouth of the lama Mañjunātha himself [in his *Condensed Exposition of the Stages of the Path*]:

> Generate properly thus the common path
> Necessary for the two superior Mahāyāna paths,
> The Perfection Vehicle, the cause, and the *Tantra* Vehicle, the effect.
> Enter the great ocean of *tantra*
> Relying on a protector, a skilful captain,
> And obtain the complete precepts.
> Make worthwhile the attainment of leisure and fortune.
> I, a yogī, practised such.
> You, wishing liberation, also do so, please.

You should turn about in your mental continuum these practices, from respecting an excellent spiritual guide properly with both thought and deed through to learning the two stages of the profound path. Practise each day in four sessions or at least one session. If so, the excellent essence will be extracted from this life of leisure. The precious teaching of the Conqueror Buddha can further the mental continuums of yourself and others.

AUTHOR'S DEDICATION: I dedicate whatever very wholesome virtues, like a conch and a jasmine, are obtained from making effort in this way in order that the teaching of the Conqueror Buddha, the sole basis of the livelihood of all beings, may remain for a long time. May this lamp of teaching perfected well with countless difficulties by Mañjunātha [Tsong-ka-pa] remain as long as this earth remains, and may it clear away the darkness of mind of all migrators. May the excellent King of Doctrine, Damcan, with his retinue who promised never to cease protecting and sustaining the teaching of Mañjunātha be a friend always to the accomplishment of this doctrine.

PRINTER'S DEDICATION: Thus, this *Instructions on the Three Principal Aspects of the Path, the Essence of All the Scriptures, the Quintessence of Helping Others* was written by the glorious and good conqueror over all sides, the Śākya monk Lo-sang-pel-den-ten-pay-nyi-ma [bLo-bzang-dpal-ldan-bstan-pa'i-nyi-ma] in a room of the Ka-dam [bKa'-gdams] mansion. By this printing may the precious teaching of Śākyamuni Buddha increase and extend in all directions.

DONOR'S DEDICATION: *Oṃ svasti.* In order that all beings might use this broad tree—being a composite of the teaching of the Conqueror Buddha, a source of help and happiness—for the good fruit of superior liberation, I established this endless river of doctrinal giving at the great doctrinal college of Tra-shi-hlun-drup [bKra-shis-lhun-grub].

Sarvajagataṃ

PART TWO

Theory: Systems of Tenets

An annotated translation of Kön-chok-jik-may-wang-po's *Precious Garland of Tenets*

Associate editor: Anne Klein

Material set in smaller type or within brackets is explanation added by the translators.

INTRODUCTION

OUR OWN AND OTHERS' PRESENTATION OF TENETS

The snowy mountain of Buddha's two marvellous collections of merit and wisdom was melted by the warmth of his compassion. The stream gathered in a circle on the earth of the spontaneous Truth Body and split into the rivers of the four schools of tenets. The successive waves of his deeds extended into space, and the childlike Forders (*Tīrthika*) were frightened. May the chief of Subduers, the great lake Manasarowar, the harbour of millions of the Conqueror's sons who are hooded dragons, prevail.

Obeisance to the regent of the Conqueror, the undaunted protector Maitreya; to the union of all the wisdom of the Conquerors, Mañjughoṣa; to the honourable Nāgārjuna and Asaṅga who were prophesied by the Conqueror; and to the second Conqueror, Tsong-ka-pa and his spiritual sons, Gyel-tsap and Kay-drup [rGyal-tshab and mKhas-grub].

If a presentation of tenets is understood, one sees all the different attributes of the outer [non-Buddhist] and inner [Buddhist] teachings and assumes the discipline of those who are the best of propounders among countless scholars. What wise person would cast aside the effort to determine the features of an arrangement of our own and others' tenets, a white banner, known to be marvellous, flown by an unbiased being!

Therefore, condensing all the good explanations of excellent beings, I will briefly put forth a presentation of tenets in order to provide for those whose lot is similar to mine. Those who seek clear understanding should listen respectfully.

Moreover, persons who are not looking for material goods and respect in this life, nor for poetry, but who seek liberation from the depths of their hearts must make effort at the means of understanding the correct view of selflessness. For, no matter how much you have internalized love, compassion, and the altruistic aspiration to enlightenment, if you are without the profound view of selflessness, you are unable to remove the root of suffering.

Love is the wish that all sentient beings be joined with happiness. Compassion is the wish that all sentient beings be separated from suffering. The altruistic aspiration to enlightenment is the wish to attain Buddhahood in order to help all sentient beings. In order to carry out these three wishes, one must overcome the cause of suffering which is the ignorance that conceives of self.

The great venerable Tsong-ka-pa said in his *Three Principal Aspects of the Path:*

If you do not have the wisdom
Realizing the way things are,
Even though you have developed the thought
Definitely to leave cyclic existence and
The altruistic aspiration to highest enlightenment,
The root of cyclic existence cannot be cut.
Therefore make effort at the means
Of realizing dependent-arising.

Thus, in order to remove faulty views and to define the gradation of coarse and subtle selflessnesses [emptinesses], I will give a brief explanation of our own and others' presentations of tenets. This explanation has two parts, a general teaching and a detailed explanation.

I. OUR OWN AND OTHERS' TENETS IN GENERAL

The expression 'tenets' (*siddhānta*) is not my own handiwork because it was mentioned in Buddha's *sūtras*. [*Sūtras* are teachings spoken by Buddha himself.] The *Descent into Laṅkā Sūtra* (*Laṅkā-vatāra-sūtra*) says:

> My doctrine has two modes,
> Advice and tenets.
> To children I speak advice
> And to yogīs, tenets.

Further, there are two types of persons: those whose minds have not been affected by tenets and those whose minds have been affected by tenets. Those whose minds have not been affected by tenets seek only the pleasures of this life with the inborn intellect which, since they have never studied a system of tenets, neither investigates nor analyses. Those whose minds have been affected by tenets are those who have studied some system. By citing scripture and reasoning they propound a way of establishing a presentation of the three—basis, paths, and fruits—which accords with their own knowledge.

The etymology for 'tenet' (*siddhānta*) is: a tenet [literally, an established conclusion] is a meaning which was made firm, decided upon, or established in reliance on scripture and/or reasoning and which will not be forsaken for something else. Dharmamitra's *Clear Words, A Commentary on* [*Maitreya's*] *'Ornament for the Realizations'* (*Abhisamayālaṃkārakārikāprajñāpāra-mitopadeśaśāstraṭikā*) says: ' "Established conclusion" [tenet] signifies one's own established assertion which is thoroughly borne out by scripture and reasoning. Because one will not pass beyond this assertion, it is a conclusion.'

Schools of tenets are divided into two types, Outsider [non-Buddhist] and Insider [Buddhist]. There is a difference between Outsiders and Insiders because a person who goes for refuge to the Three Jewels from the depths of his heart is an Insider, and a person who goes for refuge from the depths of his heart to a god of the transient world without turning his mind toward the Three Jewels is an Outsider.

The Three Jewels are Buddha, the *dharma* or realizations and abandonments that protect one from suffering and the teachings of these, and the *saṃgha* or community of Buddha's followers. These are 'jewels' (*ratna, dkon mchog*) because they are precious and difficult to find. The Tibetan term literally means 'superior rarity'; the three are superior because, possessing perfect attributes, they are similar to a wish-granting jewel; they are rare because these perfect attributes are seen only by one having a great mass of merit. Maitreya's *Sublime Science* (*Uttaratantra*) explains the epithet 'jewel' thus:

> Because their appearance is rare,
> Because they are the ornaments of beings,
> Because they are superior,
> Because they do not change,
> They are called Superior Rarities [Jewels].

The actual objects of refuge are the realizations and abandonments, specifically true cessations and true paths—the third and fourth noble truths—because these are what one practises in order to gain liberation and omniscience. The teacher of refuge is Buddha, and the friends helping one to refuge are the community, which here refers to at least four ordinary monks or nuns or refers to one Superior (*Ārya*).

Also, there is a difference between Outsider and Insider proponents of tenets because they differ from three points of view: teacher, teaching, and view. Our own Buddhist schools have three distinguishing traits:

1. they have a teacher who has extinguished all faults and completed his good qualities
2. their teachings are not harmful to any sentient being

3. they assert the view that the self is empty of being permanent, partless, and independent.

The others' schools possess three distinguishing traits which are the opposite of those:

1. their teachers have faults and have not completed their good qualities
2. their teachings harm and injure sentient beings
3. they assert the view that a permanent, partless, independent self does exist.

This does not mean that all the teachings of Outsiders are harmful to sentient beings, but that some teachings from each of their schools are harmful. For example, the teaching of animal sacrifice is harmful to beings, as are extreme ascetic practices. Also, the teaching of a self fortifies the innate sense of self that prevents liberation from cyclic existence.

II. CONDENSED EXPLANATION OF OUTSIDERS' TENETS

The definition of a proponent of Outsiders' tenets is a person who is a proponent of tenets, does not go for refuge to the Three Jewels and asserts that there is a [perfect] teacher other than the Three Jewels.

There are endless divisions of Outsiders; briefly, however, they are widely known to consist of five Schools of Philosophers, Vaiśṇava, Aiśvara, Jaina, Kāpila [Sāṃkhya], and Bārhaspatya [Cārvāka]. They are also explained as the six fundamental schools, Vaiśeṣika, Naiyāyika, Sāṃkhya, Mīmāṃsaka, Nirgrantha, and Lokāyata [Cārvāka]. The first five of these hold views of eternalism, and the last holds a view of nihilism.

VAIŚEṢIKA AND NAIYĀYIKA

The Vaiśeṣikas [Particularists] and the Naiyāyikas [Logicians] are followers of the sage Kaṇāda and the Brāhmaṇa Akṣipāda respectively. Although these two schools differ a little in the features of some of their assertions, their general tenets do not differ.

Both the Vaiśeṣikas and the Naiyāyikas assert that all objects of knowledge (*jñeya*) [all phenomena] are included among the six categories of existents.

These are substance, quality, activity, generality, particularity, and inherence. The first category, substance, is divided into the nine types: earth, water, fire, air, space, time, direction, self, and mind.

The second category, quality, has twenty-five types: (1) form, (2) taste, (3) smell, (4) touch, (5) sound, (6) number, (7) dimension,

(8) separateness, (9) conjunction, (10) disjunction, (11) otherness, (12) non-otherness, (13) consciousness, (14) pleasure, (15) pain, (16) desire, (17) hatred, (18) effort, (19) heaviness, (20) moisture, (21) heat, (22) oiliness, (23) momentum, (24) merit, (25) demerit. A quality has four features: (1) it depends on a substance, (2) it does not possess other qualities, (3) it does not act either as a cause of inherence or as a cause of non-inherence, (4) it does not depend on a sign, that is, a quality does not depend on another quality as a proof for its existence but is a proof for the existence of a substance.

The third category, activity, has five types: lifting up, putting down, contraction, extension, and going.

The fourth category, generality, is the common cause of designating terms and engaging the mind in a similar way with regard to a class of phenomena.

The fifth category, particularity, is that which differentiates one thing from another. It causes one to know that one phenomenon is different from another.

The sixth category, inherence, is a phenomenon which is the conjunction of a base and that which is based on it; it is a different entity from both the base and that which is based on it.[1]

They assert that ablutions, initiations, fasts, offerings, burnt offerings, and so forth are the paths of liberation. Through having practised yoga for some time in accordance with the quintessential instructions of a guru, a yogī comes to know the self as a thing other than the senses and so forth, and thereby sees reality. He understands the nature of the six categories of existents, and he knows the self to be an all-pervasive entity that lacks activity. He does not accumulate either virtuous or non-virtuous actions or the predispositions they establish. Because he does not accumulate new actions but extinguishes old ones, the self separates from the body, senses, mind, pleasure, pain, desire, hatred, and so forth, and does not assume a new body and senses. Thereby, the continuum of births is severed like a fire which has consumed its fuel. When the self is alone [without any of its nine qualities, desire, hatred, effort, pleasure, pain, consciousness, virtue, non-virtue, and activity], this is said to be the attainment of liberation.

SĀṂKHYA

The Sāṃkhyas [Enumerators] are followers of the sage Kapila. They assert that all objects of knowledge are enumerated in twenty-five categories [and according to Bhāvaviveka's *Blaze of Reasoning* (*Tarkajvālā*) they maintain that one is liberated through understanding the ramifications of this enumeration].[2]

The twenty-five categories are:[3]

1. person (*puruṣa*) [or self, consciousness, conscious self, mind, sentience, knower of the field]
2. fundamental nature (*prakṛti*) [or nature, principle, universality, general principle]
3. intellect (*buddhi*), or great one (*mahat*)
4. I-principle (*ahaṃkāra*)
   (*a*) I-principle dominated by activity (*rajaḥ*)
   (*b*) I-principle dominated by darkness (*tamaḥ*)
   (*c*) I-principle dominated by lightness (*sattva*).

Five subtle objects or potencies of objects which evolve from the I-principle dominated by activity:

5. forms (*rūpa*)
6. sounds (*śabda*)
7. odours (*gandha*)
8. tastes (*rasa*)
9. tangible objects (*spraṣṭavya*).

Eleven faculties which evolve from the I-principle dominated by lightness:

Five mental faculties:

10. eye (*cakṣuḥ*)
11. ear (*śrota*)
12. nose (*ghrāṇa*)
13. tongue (*rasana*)
14. body (*sparśana*).

Five physical faculties or action faculties:

15. speech (*vāc*)

16. arms (*pāṇi*)
17. legs (*pāda*)
18. anus (*pāyu*)
19. genitalia (*upastha*).

20. Intellectual faculty (*manaḥ*) the nature of which is both mental and physical.

Five elements:

21. earth (*pṛthivī*) which evolves from the odour potency
22. water (*āp*) which evolves from the taste potency
23. fire (*tejaḥ*) which evolves from the form potency
24. wind (*vāyu*) which evolves from the tangible object potency
25. space (*ākāśa*) which evolves from the sound potency.

From among these twenty-five categories, the person or self is asserted to be [just] consciousness [because it is not an aggregation of particles].[4] The remaining twenty-four are asserted to be matter because they are aggregations [of particles].[5] The person and the fundamental nature are ultimate truths (*paramārtha-satya*) [because they are non-manifest objects of knowledge].[6] The others are asserted to be conventional truths (*saṃvṛti-satya*).

Furthermore, these twenty-five categories are included in only four types: that which is a cause but not an effect; that which is both a cause and an effect; that which is an effect but not a cause; and that which is neither a cause nor an effect.

The fundamental nature is a cause but not an effect.

The intellect, the I-principle, and the five subtle objects are both causes and effects.

The remaining sixteen [the eleven faculties and the five elements] are effects but not causes.

The person is neither a cause nor an effect.

Fundamental nature, general principle, and principle are synonyms. The fundamental nature is asserted to be an object of knowledge which possesses six distinguishing characteristics.

1. It is the agent of actions because it is the agent of virtue and non-virtue.

2. It is unborn and permanent because it does not disintegrate or dissolve into anything else.
3. It is single because it is partless.
4. It is only an object and not an object-possessor, i.e. subject, because it is without realization and without consciousness and because it is the object of enjoyment of the person.
5. It pervades all animate and inanimate objects, such as cause and effect, because it pervades all transformations.
6. It is unmanifest and is an equilibrium of the three qualities: activity, lightness, and darkness.[7]

Person, self, consciousness, and mind are synonyms.

The mode of production of the remaining twenty-three is the following. Whenever the person generates a desire to enjoy objects, the fundamental nature [recognizes this desire, unites with the person[8] and] creates manifestations such as sounds.

According to the non-theistic Sāṃkhyas all manifest objects whatsoever are transformations of the fundamental nature. The theistic Sāṃkhyas assert that the varieties of environments and animate beings are not produced from the fundamental nature alone because it is mindless and that which is mindless is not capable of overseeing production. Without an overseer the initiation of an effect is not possible. The person is not suitable to be the overseer because at that time, before the transformation of the fundamental nature, there is no knowledge since the intellect has not yet been produced and without determination by the intellect there is no realization of objects. Therefore, through the mutual dependence of the great god Īśvara and the fundamental nature, the varieties of effects are produced. When from among the three qualities which dwell in the entity of the fundamental nature the quality of activity increases in strength, this acts as the cause of Īśvara's issuing forth all animate beings and environments. When lightness increases in strength, this acts as the cause of their duration. When darkness increases in strength, this acts as the cause of their disintegration. Therefore, although Īśvara and the fundamental nature, which are the two causes that produce all manifest phenomena, always exist, serial production, duration, and disintegration of effects are admissible because the three, activity, lightness, and darkness, increase and diminish serially.[9]

The intellect arises from the fundamental nature. Intellect and great one are synonyms. The intellect is considered to be like a two-sided mirror which reflects the images of objects from the outside and the image of the person from the inside.

The intellect 'empowers' the senses, and it apprehends the objects which the senses apprehend; these objects are then known by the person. The person is consciousness, and the intellect is the entity wherein consciousness mixes with the senses, which are matter.[10] The person is then mistakenly confused with the senses; this error must be corrected in order to attain liberation.

From the intellect, the I-principle is produced; it has three divisions: the activity dominated I-principle, the lightness dominated I-principle, and the darkness dominated I-principle. From the first, the activity dominated I-principle, the five subtle objects are produced, and the five elements are produced from these [see chart, p. 59]. From the second, the lightness dominated I-principle, the eleven faculties are produced. The third, the darkness dominated I-principle, is said to be the motivator of the other two.

This presentation accords with that of Tsong-ka-pa and Gyel-tsap; however, Avalokitavrata names the darkness dominated I-principle as producer of the five subtle objects and the activity dominated I-principle as the motivator of the other two I-principles.[11]

The fundamental nature which is like a blind man with good legs and the person which is like a cripple with good eyesight are mistaken to be one. The Sāṃkhyas assert that cyclic existence occurs through the force of ignorance regarding the way in which transformations are manifested by the fundamental nature. If, in dependence on hearing the quintessential instructions of a teacher, one fully generates the definite knowledge that the transformations are only manifestations of the fundamental nature, one gradually separates from attachment to objects. At that time, through relying on the concentrations, the clairvoyance of the divine eye is generated. The fundamental nature, when it is seen by this clairvoyant consciousness, is flushed with shame like another's wife [that is, like a mistress when seen by a wife]; it gathers its transformations [and disappears]. The fundamental nature then dwells alone [separate from the self] with the result that all appearances of conventional phenomena disappear for the mind of the yogī. The person then abides without enjoying objects and without action; at that time, liberation is attained.

MĪMĀṂSAKA

The Mīmāṃsakas [Analysers or Ritualists] are followers of Jaimini. They maintain that whatever appears in the *Vedas* is self-produced [because the *Vedas* were not made by anyone].

Bhāvaviveka says in his *Heart of the Middle Way* (*Madhyamakahṛdaya*): 'Because of degeneration [which occurs on account of] the faults of desire and so forth, the words of persons are always false. Because the *Vedas* were not made by persons, they are held to be valid sources of knowledge.' The scriptures of the Sāṃkhyas, Vaiśeṣikas, Nirgranthas, Nihilists, Buddhists, and so forth are false because they were made by persons.[12]

They falsely consider that what appears in the *Vedas* is reality, and, therefore, they assert that offerings and so forth [which are revealed in the *Vedas*] are the only way to attain a high condition of life [in the future].

This high condition of life is asserted to be liberation only from bad migrations [not liberation from all migrations in cyclic existence]. Moreover, there is no liberation that extinguishes all suffering; this is because defilements abide in the nature of the mind [and, therefore, to eliminate defilements would be to eliminate the mind]. Also, there is no omniscience because objects of knowledge are limitless. Hence, the Mīmāṃsakas also propound that there is no true speech [of persons; only the *Vedas* are true].

NIRGRANTHA

The Nirgranthas [Jainas] are followers of Ṛṣabha Jina. They assert that all objects of knowledge are included in nine categories: life, contamination, restraint, wearing down, bond, action, sin, merit, and liberation.

Life is self; it is the same size as a person's body. Its nature is ermanent, but its states are impermanent.

Contamination is virtuous or non-virtuous action because on account of actions one falls into cyclic existence.

Restraint is what ceases contaminations because on account of it actions are not newly accumulated.

Wearing down is exhaustion of previously accumulated action [karmic matter] by means of asceticism such as not drinking liquids, physical hardships, and so forth.

A bond is a mistaken view.

Actions are of four types: [the determiners of the general] experience in a later life, of name, of lineage, and of life-span.

Sin is non-virtue.

Merit is virtue.

Liberation is the following. By resorting to deeds of asceticism such as going naked, not speaking, the five fires [fires in front, back, on both sides, and the sun above] and so forth, all previous actions are consumed [and liberation, a state which lacks all contaminations of good and bad actions, is attained]. Because actions are not newly accumulated, one goes to a place that is at the top of all worlds, called Consummation of the Worlds. It is like a white umbrella held upside down, white like yogurt and the esculent white water lily, the size of four million five hundred thousand *yojanas*. Because this place has life, it is a thing (*bhāva*); because it is free from cyclic existence, it is also a non-thing (*abhāva*). This place is called liberation.

Ṛṣabha Jina said:

Jina explains that liberation
Has the colour of snow, the incense flower
Cow's yogurt, frost, and pearl,
The shape of a white umbrella.

CĀRVĀKA

The Cārvākas [Hedonists] say that one does not come to this life from a previous life because no one perceives previous lives. From an adventitious body a mind is adventitiously achieved, just as light is adventitiously achieved from the adventitious existence of a lamp.

Also, one does not go to a future life from this life. Body and mind are one entity; therefore, when the body perishes, the mind also perishes. For example, when a stone is destroyed, the design on the stone is likewise destroyed.

Thus, this system maintains that all objects of comprehension [all existents] are necessarily specifically characterized [i.e. directly perceived] phenomena and all valid cognizers are necessarily direct valid cognizers. This is because they do not accept that generally characterized [i.e. indirectly perceived] phenomena or inferential valid cognizers exist.

Some Cārvākas assert that all phenomena [whose causes cannot be directly perceived] arise from their own nature, causelessly. They say:

The rising of the sun, the running downwards of a river,
The roundness of peas, the sharpness of thorns,
The 'eyes' of peacock feathers and so forth—all phenomena
Arise from their own nature, without being made by anyone.

* * *

Thus I say:

A rung on the ladder to the city of liberation
Is the understanding and abandoning
Of all types of Outsiders' tenets
Being fords to extremes of bad views.

III. GENERAL EXPOSITION OF BUDDHIST TENETS

The King of the Śākyas, a peerless teacher, initially generated an attitude of dedication to attaining highest enlightenment for the sake of all sentient beings. Then, [in order to actualize this wish] he amassed the collections of merit and wisdom for three countless aeons. Finally, in the vicinity of Bodhgayā, he became perfectly enlightened.

At Varaṇāsī he turned the wheel of doctrine of the four noble truths for the five good ascetics [who had previously practised asceticism with him]. Then, on Vulture Peak [so called because it is shaped like a heap of vultures] he turned the wheel of doctrine of signlessness [that is, phenomena's lack of possessing any signs of true existence]. Then, at Vaiśālī and other places, he turned the extensive wheel of doctrine of good discrimination.

The third wheel is called the wheel of good discrimination because it discriminates well between what does and does not truly exist. The fundamental idea of the first wheel was that all phenomena without exception ultimately exist and that in this respect there is no difference or cause for discrimination among them. The fundamental idea of the second wheel was that all phenomena without exception do not ultimately exist and that in this respect there is no difference or cause for discrimination among them. When Buddha was questioned about the conflict between these two teachings, he taught the third wheel in which he explained that thoroughly established phenomena (*pariniṣpanna*), that is, emptinesses, and dependent phenomena (*paratantra*), such as houses, trees, and persons, ultimately exist, but that imaginaries (*parikalpita*), such as space and cessations, do not. Thus, the third wheel is the teaching that discriminates what does and does not ultimately exist.

This method of categorizing the three wheels of doctrine is found in the *Unravelling of the Thought Sūtra* (*Saṃdhinirmocana-sūtra*). It says that the first wheel consists of teachings of the four noble truths and the like, which were taught mainly for the sake of Hīnayāna disciples; that the second wheel consists of the *Perfection of Wisdom Sūtras* and the like, which were taught mainly for the sake of Mahāyāna disciples; and that the third wheel, which includes the *Unravelling of the Thought Sūtra* itself, was taught for the sake of both Hīnayāna and Mahāyāna disciples. The *Unravelling of the Thought Sūtra* teaches that the third wheel is the highest and most direct. However, this teaching is for Cittamātrins; the Prāsaṅgika system, which is considered to be the highest school of tenets and follows the second wheel, says that this presentation of the three wheels requires interpretation.

All inferior proponents of tenets, the six Forder (*Tīrthika*) teachers and so forth were quelled by Buddha's magnificence; and his teaching, a source of help and happiness, flourished and spread widely. Later on, commentators explained individually the thought of the three wheels, and thus the four schools of tenets arose. Of these four, the two schools which propound [truly existent external] objects [Vaibhāṣika and Sautrāntika] followed the first wheel. The proponents of no [truly existing] entityness [Mādhyamikas] followed the second wheel; and the Yogācārins followed the third wheel. All four schools make presentations of the three, basis, paths, and fruits, following their respective wheels.

The number of schools of tenets which follow our teacher is definitely four: the two Hīnayāna schools, Vaibhāṣika and Sautrāntika, and the two Mahāyāna schools, Cittamātra and Mādhyamika. This is so because it is said that there is no fifth system of tenets apart from these four and that there is no fourth vehicle apart from the three vehicles [Hearer, Solitary Realizer, and Bodhisattva vehicles]. Vajragarbha's *Commentary on the Condensation of the Hevajra Tantra* (*Hevajrapiṇḍārthaṭīkā*) says: 'It is not the Subduer's thought that a fourth [vehicle] or a fifth [school of tenets] exists for Buddhists.'

When the Svātantrika, Cittamātra, Sautrāntika, and Vaibhāṣika are weighed by the Prāsaṅgika, they are all found to fall to extremes of permanence and annihilation.

The order of the schools from top to bottom is:

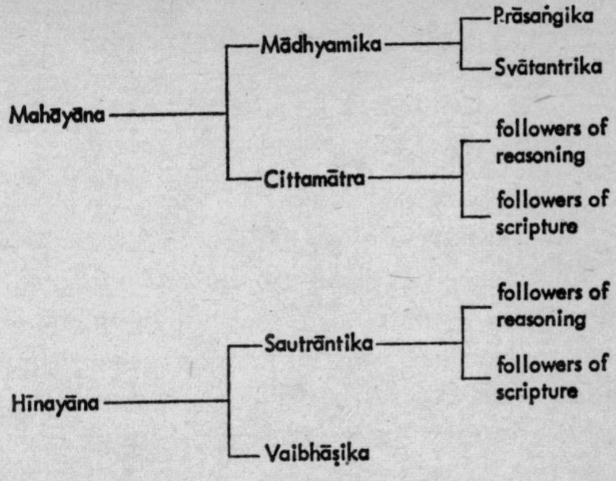

However, the Svātantrikas and below each maintain that their own system is Mādhyamika [a middle way] because they claim that they assert a middle way which is free from the two extremes of permanence and annihilation. Moreover, each of the four schools of tenets has a different way of avoiding the extremes of permanence and annihilation.

The Vaibhāṣikas maintain that they avoid the extreme of permanence because they assert that when an effect is produced, its causes cease. They say that they also avoid the extreme of annihilation because they assert that an effect arises after the termination of a cause.

The Sautrāntikas say that they avoid the extreme of annihilation through asserting that the continuum of a product exists continuously.

For example, they assert that when a table is burned, the continuum of a similar type of product—namely the continuum of a specific table—is severed but that the continuum of the substance is not severed because ashes remain.

The Sautrāntikas maintain that they are also free from the extreme of permanence because of their assertion that products disintegrate from moment to moment.

The Cittamātrins say that they avoid the extreme of permanence by asserting that imaginary phenomena do not truly exist. They say that they also avoid the extreme of annihilation through asserting the true existence of dependent phenomena.

The Mādhyamikas maintain that they are free from the extreme of annihilation because they assert the conventional existence of all phenomena. They consider that they are free from the extreme of permanence because they assert that all phenomena whatsoever are without ultimate existence.

Although those tenets of the lower schools which are not shared by the higher schools are refuted by the higher schools of tenets, an understanding of the lower views is an excellent method for gaining an understanding of the higher views. Therefore, you should not despise the lower tenets just because you hold the higher tenets to be superior.

The definition of a proponent of Buddhist tenets is: a person who asserts the four seals which are the views testifying that a doctrine is Buddha's. The four seals are:

all products are impermanent
all contaminated things are miserable
all phenomena are selfless
nirvāṇa is peace.

Products are phenomena such as chairs and tables which are produced in dependence on an aggregation of major and minor causes. Non-products are phenomena such as space that are not produced in dependence on major or minor causes. Contaminated things are those phenomena which are under the influence of contaminated actions and afflictions. Phenomena are selfless in the sense that they are empty of being a permanent, partless, independent self or of being the objects of use of such a self. *Nirvāṇa* is peace because peace is not bestowed by Indra, or anyone else, but is achieved by one's own individual passing beyond the afflictions of desire, hatred, and ignorance.

Someone might say: In that case, the Vātīsputrīyas [a Vaibhāṣika subschool] would not be proponents of Buddhist tenets because they assert a self of persons. No, there is no such fallacy. The self which they assert is a substantially existent or self-sufficient self whereas the selflessness of the Buddhist four seals refers to the absence of a permanent, partless, independent self. Furthermore, such a self [as mentioned in the four seals] is not asserted by the five Saṃmitīya schools [although they do assert an inexpressible self].

The tenets of the four schools and their subschools are discussed in detail in chapters IV to VIII.

IV. THE VAIBHĀṢIKAS

DEFINITION, SUBSCHOOLS AND ETYMOLOGY

The definition of a Vaibhāṣika is: a person propounding Hīnayāna tenets who does not accept self-consciousness (*svasaṃvedanā*) and who asserts external objects as being truly existent.

Self-consciousness is a mind's awareness of itself simultaneous with its awareness of an object.

There are three groups of Vaibhāṣikas: Kashmiris, Aparāntakas, and Magadhas.

There is reason for calling the teacher Vasumitra a Vaibhāṣika because he propounds tenets following the *Great Detailed Explanation* (*Mahāvibhāṣā*) and because he propounds that the three times [past, present, and future objects] are instances of substantial entities.

PRESENTATION OF THE BASIS

This section has two parts, assertions regarding objects and assertions regarding object-possessors [subjects].

Assertions regarding objects

This system asserts that all objects of knowledge are included within five basic categories: appearing forms (*rūpa*), main minds (*citta*), accompanying mental factors (*caitta*), compositional factors which are not associated with either minds or mental factors (*citta-caitta-viprayukta-saṃskāra*), and non-products (*asaṃskṛta*).

Forms are of eleven types: the five sense objects, the five sense powers, and non-revelatory forms. The five sense objects are: (1) colours and shapes, (2) sounds, (3) odours, (4) tastes, and (5) tangible objects. The five sense powers are: (6) eye sense, (7) ear sense, (8) nose sense, (9) tongue sense, and (10) body sense. Non-revelatory forms are, for example, the subtle form of the absence of a vow as in the case of the subtle form of non-virtuous deeds that a butcher would always possess even when not actually engaged in killing.

A main mind is a consciousness apprehending the general object, such as an eye consciousness which apprehends a table. Mental factors accompany main minds, and apprehend the particulars of an object, for example, the pleasantness or unpleasantness of a table. Ten mental factors accompany all main minds: feeling, intention, discrimination, aspiration, contact, intelligence, mindfulness, mental activity, interest, and stabilization. Examples of products which are not associated with minds or mental factors are the four characteristics of products: production, ageing, duration, and disintegration. Etymologically speaking, these are phenomena which are not associated (*viprayukta*) with minds or mental factors; however, they are neither form nor consciousness.

These five objects are 'things' (*bhāva*). The definition of a thing is: that which is able to perform a function. Existent (*sat*), object of knowledge (*jñeya*), and thing are synonymous. Non-products are considered to be permanent things; forms, consciousnesses, and non-associated compositional factors [which are neither form nor consciousness] are considered to be impermanent things.

This system asserts that a non-product such as a space is able to perform a function and thus is a thing. For instance, the lack of obstructing contact that a space affords allows movement to take place.

All things are necessarily substantially established entities (*dravya-siddha*) but they are not necessarily substantially existent (*dravya-sat*). This is so because they assert that 'ultimate truth' and 'substantial existent' are synonyms and that 'conventional truth' and 'imputed existent' are synonyms.

There is a division of objects into the two truths and into the contaminated and non-contaminated. Also [with regard to this discussion of objects] there is a teaching of other ancillary topics.

The two truths. The definition of a conventional truth is: a phenomenon which is such that if it were broken up or mentally separated into parts, the consciousness apprehending that object would be cancelled. A clay pot and a rosary are examples of conventional truths because, if a clay pot is broken with a hammer, the mind which apprehends that object as a clay pot is cancelled; and, if the beads of a rosary are separated, the mind which apprehends that object as a rosary is cancelled.

The definition of an ultimate truth is: a phenomenon which is such that if it were broken up or mentally separated into parts, the consciousness apprehending that object would not be cancelled. Examples of ultimate truths are directionally partless particles, temporally partless moments of consciousness, and the space which is a non-product.

The smallest units of matter are directionally partless, but this does not mean that they are partless in general; even the smallest particle has factors relating to its production, duration, and cessation and factors relating to the production of effects, and so forth. Similarly, the smallest temporal unit of consciousness is temporally partless but is not partless in general; for, one instant of an eye consciousness can have many parts which apprehend the various colours of, for instance, a tile floor.

The *Treasury of Knowledge* (*Abhidharmakośa*) says: 'A thing which if broken or mentally separated into others [i.e. parts] is then no longer understood by the mind [to be that thing], such as a pot or water, is conventionally existent. All others are ultimately existent.' Therefore, it is asserted that conventional truths are not ultimately existent, although they are truly existent. This is because this system asserts that all things are truly existent.

The contaminated and the non-contaminated. The definition of a contaminated object is: a phenomenon which is amenable to the increase of contaminations from the point of view of being either an object of awareness or an afflicted concomitant. The five mental and physical aggregates (*skandha*) are examples of contaminated objects.

However, not all phenomena included in the five mental and physical aggregates are examples of contaminated phenomena because true paths—the fourth of the four noble truths—are included in the five aggregates but are not contaminated objects.

A table, for example, is a contaminated phenomenon not because it possesses the afflictions of desire, hatred, or ignorance but because it can act as an object of awareness that increases those afflictions, especially desire, in the perceiver. An afflicted concomitant can be an afflicted main mind that accompanies afflicted mental factors or an afflicted mental factor that accompanies an afflicted main mind or other afflicted mental factors. An example is the mental factor of desire which accompanies the perception of an attractive object and could increase the afflictions of the main mind and other mental factors which accompany it.

All phenomena which are contaminated from the point of view of being afflicted concomitants are also contaminated from the point of view of being objects of awareness because they can increase afflictions in other beings who take cognizance of them, or they can increase one's own afflictions if one should take cognizance of them at a later time, as in the case of desire. However, all phenomena which are contaminated objects from the point of view of being objects of awareness are not necessarily contaminated from the point of view of being afflicted concomitants, such as an attractive table which could never be an afflicted concomitant because it is not a mind or a mental factor.

The definition of a non-contaminated object is: a phenomenon which is not amenable to the increase of contaminations from the point of view of being either an object of awareness or a mental concomitant. True paths and non-products are examples, for, the *Treasury of Knowledge* says, 'Except for true paths, all products are contaminated'; and, 'The non-contaminated consists of true paths and the three non-products.'

When true paths are objects of awareness or mental concomitants, they destroy contamination and do not increase it. A space as an object of awareness cannot destroy contamination, but does not increase it. The three non-products are: non-analytical cessations, analytical cessations, and spaces. A non-analytical cessation is a cessation which occurs as a result of the incompleteness of the causes for its production, such as the lack of hunger at the time of intensely concentrating on studies. Once the moment has passed, the fact that one had no desire for food at that time will never change, and for this reason, its cessation is said to be permanent. An analytical cessation is an eradication of an obstruction such that it will never occur again, as in the case of a complete cessation forever of a particular type of desire through meditation on the four noble truths.

All contaminated objects are to be abandoned, for even the two paths, accumulation and preparation (*saṃbhāra-mārga* and *prayoga-mārga*), are to be abandoned.

The paths of accumulation and preparation are not actual antidotes to afflictions and thus do not eliminate afflictions; they are virtues of common beings and, therefore, suitable to increase desire.

The path of seeing (*darśana-mārga*) is completely non-contaminated.

The path of seeing consists solely of direct contemplation of the four truths and occurs only in one meditative session; thus, it is only non-contaminated.

Paths of meditation (*bhāvanā-mārga*) and paths of no more learning (*aśaikṣa-mārga*) both have instances of contaminated and non-contaminated paths.

On both the path of meditation and the path of no more learning there are instances when yogīs cultivate worldly paths such as the eight absorptions for the sake of increasing their mental capacity. These worldly paths are paths of meditation. They are contaminated from the point of view of being objects of awareness because, through taking cognizance of them, afflictions not only are not eliminated but also are suitable to increase in the sense that someone could become desirous of these paths. One who has attained the path of no more learning no longer has any afflictions; therefore, his training in the eight absorptions could not increase afflictions for him, but these worldly paths could increase the desire of others who notice them. Worldly paths in the continuum of one who has attained the path of no more learning are, therefore, contaminated from the point of view of being objects of awareness but not from the point of view of being afflicted concomitants because they themselves are not afflicted in the sense that desire, for instance, is afflicted.

All superior (*ārya*) paths are necessarily non-contaminated, but the paths in the continuum of a Superior are not necessarily non-contaminated. This is because a path which is in the continuum of one on the path of meditation and which has the aspect of reflecting on the subtlety [of higher levels] and the coarseness [of the present level] is contaminated [as in the case of generating the eight absorptions].

All Buddhist schools except the Vaibhāṣika and the Sautrāntika following scripture maintain that a superior path and a path in the continuum of a Superior are synonymous. The Vaibhāṣikas state the example of one who meditates on the advantages of the first concentration, such as peacefulness and long life, and on the disadvantages of the desire realm, such as coarseness, ugliness, and short life, in order to do away with manifest desire for the objects of the desire realm. By meditating thus a yogī can attain a higher state of concentration and can suppress manifest afflictions, but he cannot get rid of the seeds of the afflictions. Many non-Buddhists attain their 'liberation' through this means; however, because of the fault of not destroying the seeds of desire by means of analytical cessation, such 'liberation' is only temporary. In the specific case mentioned in the text, the meditator is a Superior on the path of meditation. On this path those of greater intelligence simultaneously rid themselves of the afflictions together with their seeds, level by level in nine stages (see chart p. 88). However, the Superior being discussed here is one of duller faculties and suppresses manifest afflictions first; only afterwards does he go on to rid himself of the seeds of those afflictions.

Other ancillary topics. The three times [past, present, and future objects] are asserted to be substantial entities because the Vaibhāṣikas maintain that a pot exists even at the time of the past of a pot and that a pot exists even at the time of the future of a pot.

Yesterday's pot exists today as a past pot. The past of a thing occurs after its present existence, that is, after its present existence has passed. Tomorrow's pot exists today as a future pot. The future of a thing occurs before its present existence, that is, when its present existence is yet to be. Today's pot exists as a present pot today.

Although they assert that both negative phenomena and affirmative phenomena exist, they do not accept the existence of non-affirming negatives because they consider that all negatives are necessarily affirming negatives.

An affirmative phenomenon such as a 'table' does not require the explicit negation of its being non-table in order for that table to appear to the mind, but a negative phenomenon such as 'non-table' entails an explicit negation of table in order for it to appear to the mind. The Vaibhāṣikas consider that there is always something affirmative about a negative because their system always deals with substantial entities. This emphasis on substantiality sets in relief the tendency of the higher schools to become less and less substance oriented, and these variations are especially significant as regards the schools' different modes of arriving at their interpretations of emptiness.

The Kashmiri Vaibhāṣikas accord with the Sautrāntikas in asserting that the continuum of the mental consciousness is the base that connects actions (*karma*) with their effects.

Every Buddhist system has to deal with the problem of providing for an uninterrupted base to connect karmic cause with karmic fruit. The Kashmiris say that the continuum of the mental consciousness is the base which allows the continued chain of actions and their fruits to prevail from life to life. This is because the mental consciousness, unlike the other five consciousnesses, functions even in deep sleep and during meditative equipoise.

All Vaibhāṣikas, except for the Kashmiris, assert that an obtainer (*prāpti*), a product which is neither form nor consciousness, is the base that connects actions with their fruits. This is a preventer of loss, like a seal that guarantees a loan [preventing the loan from becoming a loss to the loaner].

Both this system and the Prāsaṅgika system assert that actions of body and speech have form.

Other systems assert them to be mental. The Vaibhāṣikas and Prāsaṅgikas reason that speech is sound and that sound is form; therefore, speech is form. Also, there is coarse and subtle form. Speech which has coarse form is, for example, that heard when a person speaks. Speech which has subtle form is, for example, the pure speech manifested by a monk who, even when silent, is keeping his vow not to speak lies and so forth. Although unheard by either himself or others it nevertheless exists. Examples of bodily action which has subtle form are the ethical deeds of a Superior in meditative equipoise. These would not be seen by others, but could be seen by someone with high clairvoyance, such as a Buddha.

The Sautrāntikas, Cittamātrins, and Svātantrikas maintain that deeds of body and speech are actually mental factors of intention.

All products are necessarily impermanent but do not necessarily disintegrate moment by moment, for the Vaibhāṣikas assert that following production there is the activity of duration, and then the activity of disintegration occurs.

All Buddhist schools agree that coarse impermanence is the production of a thing such as a table, its lasting for a period of time, and finally its disintegration such as its being consumed by fire. Buddhist schools also assert a subtle impermanence which, except for developed yogīs, is not accessible to direct experience. For example, death, which is an instance of coarse impermanence, is clearly experienced, but the momentary ageing of a person, which is a subtle impermanence, is not. The Vaibhāṣikas differ from the other Buddhist schools in asserting that the factors of production, abiding, ageing, and disintegration are external to the entity which undergoes these. All other systems hold that production itself is a cause or sufficient condition for disintegration; disintegration begins with the very first moment of production. In all systems except the Vaibhāṣika, that which is produced is that which abides and that which disintegrates. This is because production is understood to be the arising of a new entity due to certain causes; abiding is the continued existence of that type of entity; disintegration is its quality of not lasting a second moment; and ageing is the factor of its being a different entity from the entity of the previous moment.

Assertions regarding object-possessors [subjects]

This section has three parts: the Vaibhāṣikas' assertions regarding persons, consciousnesses, and terms.

Every consciousness has an object and thus is an object-possessor. Every name or term expresses a meaning which is its object, and thus is an object-possessor. Every person possesses objects and is an object-possessor in that sense.

Persons. A person is the mere collection of the mental and physical aggregates (*skandha*) which are its basis of imputation. Some of the five Saṃmitīya subschools assert that each of the five aggregates is an instance of a person, and the Avantakas assert that the mind alone is an instance of a person.

Consciousnesses. This section has two parts, the Vaibhāṣikas' assertions regarding new valid consciousnesses (*pramāṇa-buddhi*) and assertions regarding non-new valid consciousnesses (*apramāṇa-buddhi*).

Consciousness is used here as a general term referring both to minds and mental factors.

NEW VALID CONSCIOUSNESSES

There are direct new valid cognizers (*pratyakṣa-pramāṇa*) and inferential new valid cognizers (*anumāṇa-pramāṇa*).

Buddhist psychological terms which signify the perceiver that perceives an object are often rendered in English by words like 'perception'. 'Perception', however, tends to indicate either the act or object of perception rather than the agent of perception; therefore, terms such as 'cognizer' and 'perceiver' are used here.

With regard to direct new valid cognizers they assert sense direct perceivers, mental direct perceivers, and yogic direct perceivers [such as direct cognizers of the four noble truths and their sixteen attributes, impermanence and so forth]. They do not accept self-consciousness as a direct perceiver.

Sense direct perceivers are the five sense consciousnesses. For a brief discussion of mental direct perceivers see p. 95. Self-consciousness refers to a consciousness simultaneously aware of its object and of its perception of that object. It is that part of a consciousness which is aware of its own cognizing activity; all systems which accept this type of consciousness assert that it is the same entity as the consciousness itself and that it cognizes the consciousness in a non-dualistic manner. For this reason, self-consciousness is rejected by the Vaibhāṣikas, Sautrāntikas following scripture, Sautrāntika-Svātantrikas, and Prāsaṅgikas, for they maintain that agent and object would be confused if such existed. The other schools assert the existence of self-consciousness mainly on the basis of common experience in which the seer of an object is remembered as well as the object that was seen, thus showing that the subjective element is aware of itself. For, if the subjective element were not aware of itself, there would be no memory of the subjective side of a cognition.

[Unlike the other schools] the Vaibhāṣikas assert that a sense direct valid cognizer is not necessarily a consciousness because a physical eye sense has the three qualities of being matter [not consciousness], of being a perceiver, and of being a valid cognizer.

They do not assert that a sense power (*indriya*) alone can perceive an object, nor do they assert that a sense consciousness alone is capable of perceiving an object. They maintain that the two together perceive an object; and consequently they, unlike all other schools, assert that both sense powers and sense consciousnesses are perceivers.

They assert that a sense consciousness knows its object nakedly, without taking on the aspect of that object. Also, they assert that a physical eye sense which is the base [of an eye consciousness] perceives form, for it is claimed that if a consciousness alone were the seer, then one would see forms which are obstructed by walls and so forth.

Because a consciousness does not have form, it is not obstructed by form; however, because the support of the eye consciousness is a physical sense power, the seer also incorporates form and so is obstructed by form.

A mind and its mental factors are asserted to be different entities.

A mind and its accompanying mental factors are each instances of consciousness and possess five similar qualities. An example of this is an inferential consciousness which cognizes that a sound is an impermanent thing. Here the main mind is a mental consciousness, and the accompanying mental factors include the ten omnipresent factors: feeling, intention, discrimination, aspiration, contact, intelligence, mindfulness, mental activity, interest, and stabilization. The five qualities which this mind and its accompanying mental factors would share are: (1) they have the same basic object, the sound; (2) they have the same 'aspect object', the impermanent sound; (3) they have the same sense as their base, namely, the mental sense which is a previous moment of the mental consciousness; (4) they are simultaneous; (5) their entities are the same in number—the mental consciousness is only one and the feeling, for instance, that accompanies it is only one. Only the Vaibhāṣikas say that a mind and its mental factors are different entities; the other schools assert that they are the same entity.

NON-NEW VALID CONSCIOUSNESSES

Non-new valid consciousnesses are perverse consciousness and so forth.

There are five types of consciousness which are not new incontrovertible cognizers: perverse consciousness, doubt re-cognition, belief, and a consciousness to which an object appears without being noticed (see pp. 101–3).

Terms. Mere sounds in general are divided into two types, sounds created from elements conjoined with consciousness and sounds created from elements not conjoined with consciousness. An example of the first is the voice of a sentient being. An example of the second is the sound of a river.

Sounds created from elements conjoined with consciousness and sounds created from elements not conjoined with consciousness are each divided into two types: sounds which intentionally indicate meaning to sentient beings and sounds which do not intentionally indicate meaning to sentient beings.

An example of a sound created from elements conjoined with consciousness which intentionally indicates meaning is the spoken expression 'house'. An example of a sound created from elements conjoined with consciousness which does not intentionally indicate meaning is the sound of a spontaneous hiccup. An example of a sound created from elements not conjoined with consciousness which intentionally indicates meaning is the sound of the great drum in the Heaven of the Thirty-Three which conveys the message of impermanence and so forth to its listeners. An example of a sound created from elements not conjoined with consciousness which does not intentionally indicate meaning is the sound of an ordinary running brook.

Sound which intentionally indicates meaning to sentient beings, sound which reveals meaning through speech, and expressive sound are synonymous. Sound which does not intentionally indicate meaning, sound which does not reveal meaning through speech, and non-expressive sound are all synonyms.

This requires qualification because there are sounds which intentionally indicate meaning to sentient beings, such as the sound of the drum in the Heaven of the Thirty-Three, but are not sounds that reveal meaning through speech.

The word of Buddha (*Buddhavacana*) and the treatises (*śāstra*) are both asserted to be entities that are collections of letters, stems, and words. They are accepted as generic images of sounds and as non-associated compositional factors. Therefore, one wonders whether in this system form and non-associated compositional factor are not mutually exclusive.

The author is wondering whether the Vaibhāṣikas assert that the sounds heard from the mouth of Buddha, which are forms, are not the word of Buddha, for the word of Buddha is comprised of the generic images of the sounds which appeared to Buddha's mind before he expressed the particular sounds. For instance, before one says the word 'tree' the generic image of the sound 'tree' first appears, and then the sound is spoken. This image of the sound 'tree' is asserted to be a non-associated compositional factor and thus neither form nor consciousness. The author is not wondering whether the Vaibhāṣikas assert that one thing could be both a form (e.g. a sound) and a non-associated compositional factor because it is clear that in the Vaibhāṣika system form and non-associated compositional factor are mutually exclusive. He is wondering whether the Vaibhāṣikas would say that the sounds heard from the mouth of Buddha are not the word of Buddha.

PRESENTATION OF PATHS

This section has three parts, the Vaibhāṣikas' assertions regarding objects of the paths, objects abandoned by the paths, and the nature of the paths.

Objects of the paths

The objects contemplated are the sixteen attributes of the four truths, impermanence and so forth.

There are four attributes to each of the four truths. The attributes of the first, true sufferings, are impermanence, misery, emptiness, and selflessness. The attributes of the second, true origins, are cause, origin, strong production, and condition. The attributes of the third, true cessations, are cessation, pacification, auspiciousness, and definite emergence from a portion of the obstructions. The attributes of the fourth, true paths, are path, knowledge, achievement, and deliverance.

Subtle selflessness and subtle selflessness of persons (*pudgala-nairātmya*) are asserted to be synonymous.

All selflessnesses are either of persons or of phenomena, and since the Vaibhāṣikas do not assert a selflessness of phenomena (*dharma-nairātmya*), for them a subtle selflessness is a selflessness of persons.

The subtle selflessness of persons is asserted to be a person's emptiness of being substantially existent or self-sufficient. From among the eighteen subschools of the Vaibhāṣikas, the five Saṃmitīya subschools do not assert that a person's emptiness of being substantially existent or self-sufficient is the subtle selflessness because they consider that a substantially existent or self-sufficient person exists.

The Vaibhāṣikas do not assert a presentation of coarse and subtle selflessnesses of phenomena because they hold that all established bases [such as mind, body, house and so on] have a self of phenomena [that is, they truly exist and have a difference of entity of subject and object].

When the Vaibhāṣikas speak of a subtle self of persons, they mean a person which is seen as having a character different from the mental and physical aggregates. This definition of 'self' applies only to persons because phenomena are not conceived this way. Therefore, within the context of their own perspective it is possible for the Vaibhāṣikas to maintain the existence of a self of phenomena, such as their true existence, and to deny the existence of a self of persons.

Objects abandoned by the paths

There are two types of ignorance to be abandoned through the path: afflicted ignorance and non-afflicted ignorance.

The first, afflicted ignorance, mainly prevents the attainment of liberation. Examples of afflicted ignorance are the conception of a self of persons and the three poisons [desire, hatred, and ignorance] which arise on account of this conception, as well as their seeds.

Non-afflicted ignorance mainly prevents the attainment of all-knowingness. Examples of non-afflicted ignorance are the four causes of non-knowingness, such as the non-afflicted obstruction that is the ignorance of the profound and subtle qualities of a Buddha.

The other three causes of non-knowingness are ignorance due to the distant place of the object, ignorance due to the distant time of the object, and ignorance due to the nature of the object, such as the subtle details of the relationship of causes with their effects.

The all-knowingness mentioned here is not a Buddha's quality of omniscience as it is understood by the Mahāyānists. All-knowingness here simply means that if a Buddha thinks about objects, seen or unseen, he will know those things one by one. The Mahāyānists, however, assert that a Buddha can know all things simultaneously and instantaneously, without exerting any effort of thought. The Vaibhāṣikas do not accept such omniscience, and, therefore, they do not assert obstructions to omniscience; they merely distinguish between afflicted and non-afflicted ignorance. The Mahāyānists distinguish between an ignorance which is an afflictive obstruction and a non-afflicted ignorance which is an obstruction to omniscience.

With respect to the obstructions, aside from the obstructions to liberation and the non-afflicted ignorance the Vaibhāṣikas do not accept the designation 'obstructions to omniscience'.

Nature of the paths

With respect to the paths of the three vehicles [Hearer, Solitary Realizer, and Bodhisattva] they assert a presentation of the five paths—path of accumulation, path of preparation, path of seeing, path of meditation, and path of no more learning; however, they do not accept the wisdoms of the ten [Bodhisattva] grounds.

They assert that the first fifteen moments of the sixteen moments of forbearance and knowledge constitute the path of seeing, and that the sixteenth moment, which is called subsequent knowledge of the path, is [the beginning of] the path of meditation [see chart, opposite].

The path of seeing is the time when direct cognition of the four noble truths occurs. The paths of forbearance are so called because one develops facility or non-fear with respect to the object of meditation; they are also called uninterrupted paths because they lead without interruption into paths of liberation in the same meditative sitting. These paths of liberation are the paths of knowledge, or the knowledge that certain afflictions have been abandoned.

Therefore, they assert that the generation [of these sixteen moments] occurs no other way than serially [one step at a time], like a goat walking over a bridge.

They envision the process in this way. The four noble truths are the objects which are contemplated on the path of seeing. For each noble truth there is a path of forbearance and a path of knowledge in relation to the desire realm (*kāma-dhātu*); there is also a path of subsequent forbearance and a path of subsequent knowledge in relation to the higher realms, the form and formless realms (*rūpa-dhātu, ārūpya-dhātu*) which are here included in one category. When the meditator completes the paths of the first truth in relation to the desire realm, he then passes on to the paths of the first truth in relation to the form and formless realms. These are the first four moments, and he proceeds like this through the sixteenth moment, which is called subsequent knowledge of the path in relation to the form and formless realms. This sixteenth moment is the time of entering the path of meditation. Other schools say that the eight forbearances can occur simultaneously and that the eight knowledges can occur simultaneously.

True paths are not necessarily consciousnesses because the Vaibhāṣikas maintain that the five non-contaminated mental and physical aggregates are true paths.

Except for the Vaibhāṣika and the Sautrāntika following scripture, all schools assert that true paths are consciousnesses. The Vaibhāṣikas include within true paths the five mental and physical aggregates at, for example, the time of the fifteenth moment of the path of seeing. However, it is not the case that every instance of the five aggregates included within a Superior's continuum is a true path and hence non-contaminated. The point is that there are instances of each of the aggregates that are true paths and thus non-contaminated. These non-contaminated phenomena are those associated with a Superior's non-contaminated path. Examples are his mental consciousness, the accompanying mental factors of feeling and discrimination, the subtle forms which restrain certain faults and which naturally arise whenever a Superior is in meditative equipoise on a non-contaminated path, and the predispositions established by his path. All these are non-contaminated objects and are true paths.

SIXTEEN MOMENTS OF FORBEARANCE AND KNOWLEDGE (read from bottom to top)

Path	Moment	Realm	Truth
path of meditation (Abider in the fruit of Stream Winner)	16 subsequent knowledge	higher realms	true paths
path of seeing (Enterer to the fruit of Stream Winner)	15 subsequent forbearance	higher realms	true paths
	14 knowledge	desire realm	true paths
	13 forbearance	desire realm	true paths
	12 subsequent knowledge	higher realms	true cessations
	11 subsequent forbearance	higher realms	true cessations
	10 knowledge	desire realm	true cessations
	9 forbearance	desire realm	true cessations
	8 subsequent knowledge	higher realms	true origins
	7 subsequent forbearance	higher realms	true origins
	6 knowledge	desire realm	true origins
	5 forbearance	desire realm	true origins
	4 subsequent knowledge	higher realms	true sufferings
	3 subsequent forbearance	higher realms	true sufferings
	2 knowledge	desire realm	true sufferings
	1 forbearance	desire realm	true sufferings

PRESENTATION OF THE FRUITS OF THE PATHS

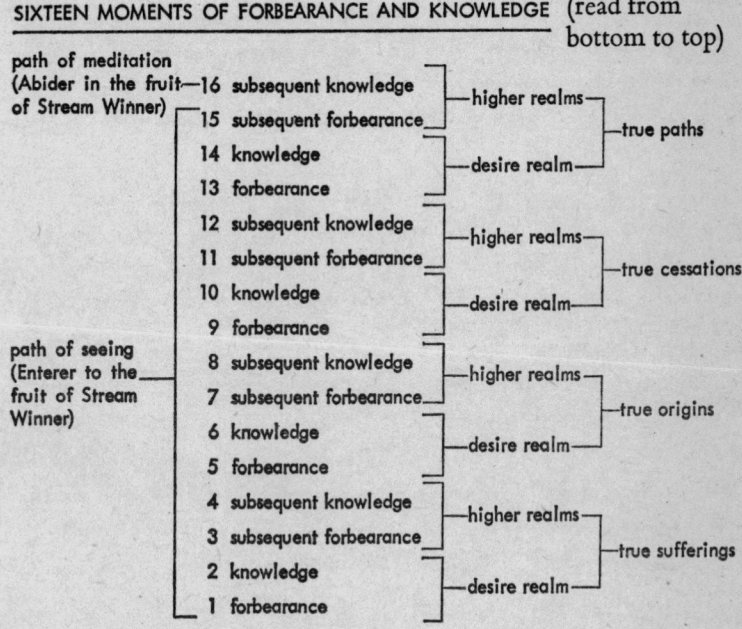

Those of the Hearer lineage become familiar with the sixteen attributes [of the four noble truths], impermanence and so forth, during three lifetimes or more. By relying on the *vajra*-like meditative stabilization of the Hearer path of meditation, they finally abandon the afflictive obstructions by ceasing their obtaining causes [potentialities which cause one to have those afflictions]. They then manifest the fruit of becoming a Foe Destroyer (*Arhan*).

On the great path of accumulation and below, a rhinoceros-like Solitary Realizer grows adept in the realization that the person is empty of substantial or self-sufficient existence. He does this in conjunction with amassing a collection of merit for one hundred aeons and so forth; and then, in one sitting, he actualizes the stages from the heat level of the path of preparation through to and including the path of no more learning.

Solitary Realizers are those who have met with teachers and listened to their teaching of the doctrine in previous lives but in their final life live in the desire realm peacefully and by themselves, like a rhinoceros. They do not meet with teachers or study doctrine in that life. Mahāyānists also assert another type of Solitary Realizer who does meet and study with a teacher in his final lifetime but later achieves his goal alone.

The Vaibhāṣikas assert the existence of types of Foe Destroyers who degenerate, because there are Hīnayāna Foe Destroyers who fall from their abandonment of the obstructions and their realizations of the four truths and thereby become Stream Winners.

The Vaibhāṣikas maintain that there are five types of fallible Foe Destroyers and a sixth type who is not capable of degeneration. Only this sixth type would be considered an actual Foe Destroyer by the other schools.

With respect to Hearers, they enumerate a presentation of the twenty members of the spiritual community (*saṃgha*) along with the eight Enterers and Abiders; however, they do not assert that anyone simultaneously [abandons the afflictions].

The twenty members of the spiritual community represent a classification of the location and number of lives remaining for practitioners on the way to attaining the fruits of Stream Winner, Once Returner, Never Returner, and Foe Destroyer.

The Eight Enterers and Abiders are beings who are approaching to or abiding in the fruits of Stream Winner, Once Returner, Never

Returner, or Foe Destroyer. The four Abiders refer to persons who have fully accomplished, or who abide in, these fruits. A Stream Winner is one who will never again be reborn as a hell-being, hungry ghost, or animal. A Once Returner will be reborn once more in the desire realm. A Never Returner will never be born again in the desire realm. A Foe Destroyer has overcome the afflictions and thus is completely liberated from cyclic existence.

Cyclic existence is divided into three realms and nine levels. The first level is the desire realm. The next four levels are the four divisions of the form realm, called the four concentrations. The last four levels are the divisions of the formless realm, called the four formless absorptions. Each level has nine series of obstacles which are to be abandoned: big big, middle big, and small big; big middle, middle middle, and small middle; big small, middle small, and small small (see chart p. 88). Thus, if the trainee proceeds serially, he would have to pass through eighty-one steps, that is, through a series of nine steps on each of the nine levels. Simultaneous abandonment refers to the simultaneous overcoming or abandoning of, for example, each of the big big of the nine levels. Thus, one who passes through the path of meditation with simultaneous abandonment has only nine steps to accomplish instead of eighty-one. The Vaibhāṣikas do not accept any such simultaneous abandonment.

They maintain that the eight types of Enterers and Abiders are necessarily Superiors.

This means that even an Enterer to the fruit of Stream Winner has attained the path of seeing, from which point he is no longer an ordinary being but a Superior. Other systems maintain that an Enterer to the fruit of Stream Winner is on the path of preparation.

A Bodhisattva [such as Śākyamuni] completes his collections [of merit and wisdom] over three countless great aeons during the path of accumulation. Having done this, he achieves the causes of the excellent marks over one hundred aeons, and then, in his final life he vanquishes the array of demons at twilight while seated beside the tree of enlightenment. At midnight, while in meditative equipoise, he actualizes the three paths of preparation, seeing, and meditation. Later, just prior to dawn, he actualizes the path of no more learning [and becomes a Buddha].

PATH OF MEDITATION (ad from bottom to top)

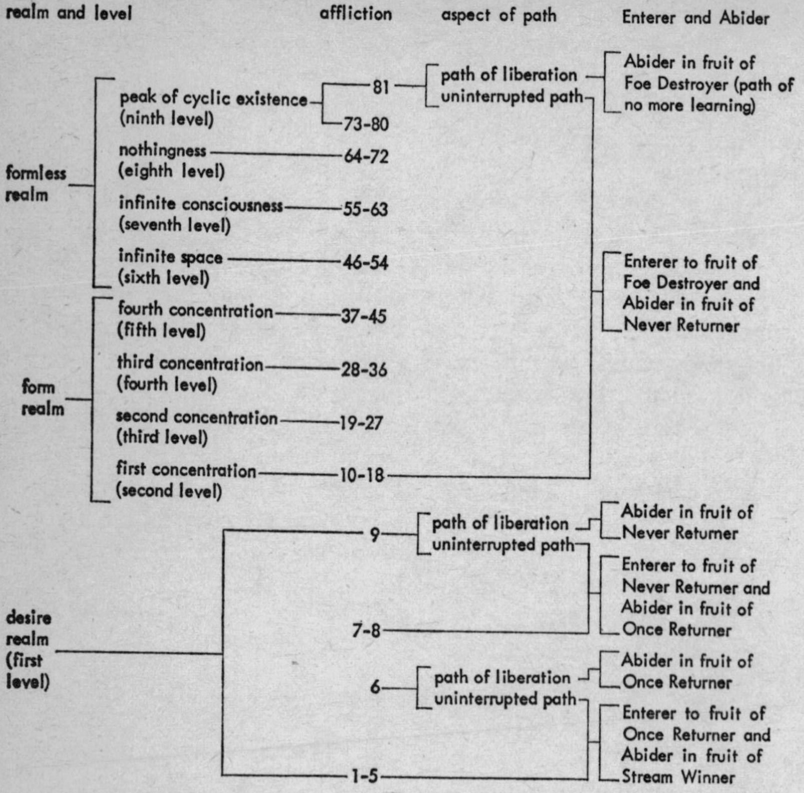

Therefore [from among the twelve deeds of a Buddha] they consider that the taming of the demons at twilight and the preceding deeds are performed when he is a common being and that the three Bodhisattva paths of preparation, seeing, and meditation are all only meditative equipoise [because they occur only during meditative sitting]. Of the twelve deeds, the first nine are asserted to be the deeds of a Bodhisattva, and the last three are asserted to be the deeds of a Buddha.

The twelve deeds are: descent from the Joyous Pure Land (*Tuṣita*), conception, birth, mastery of the arts, sporting with the retinue, renunciation, asceticism, meditation under the tree of enlightenment, conquest of the array of demons, becoming a Buddha, turning the wheel of doctrine, and *nirvāṇa*.

The Vaibhāṣikas assert that a cognitive wheel of doctrine is necessarily a path of seeing and that a verbal wheel of doctrine is necessarily a wheel of doctrine of the four truths.

The Vaibhāṣikas assert that the seven sections of *Knowledge* (*Abhidharma*) were spoken by Buddha [and written down by Foe Destroyers]. They say that Buddha's word is always literal. Apart from the eighty thousand bundles of doctrine, they do not assert a presentation of eighty-four thousand bundles of doctrine. Vasubandhu's *Treasury of Knowledge* states: 'These eighty thousand bundles of doctrine which were spoken by the Subduer . . .'

The doctrine is arranged into bundles like wheat which has been cut and bound at harvest time. A bundle signifies a teaching of variable length which, if thoroughly realized, is capable of overcoming one affliction. Those schools asserting eighty-four thousand bundles say that there are twenty-one thousand bundles for each of the three afflictions, desire, hatred, and ignorance, and a fourth bundle of twenty-one thousand for the three of these together.

The place where a Bodhisattva actualizes enlightenment during his last lifetime is definitely just the desire realm; therefore, the Vaibhāṣikas do not assert a presentation of an Enjoyment Body (*Saṃbhogakāya*), nor do they assert the existence of the Heavily Adorned Highest Pure Land (*Akaniṣṭa*).

According to the Mahāyāna systems a Highest Pure Land is where an immortal Enjoyment Body resides and preaches the Mahāyāna path to Bodhisattvas on the path of seeing and above. Ordinary beings are not found in this type of pure land although they do exist in the pure lands of Emanation Bodies (*Nirmāṇakāya*).

Not only this, but they also do not accept omniscience [because they only assert all-knowingness as mentioned above].

All Foe Destroyers of the three vehicles have a *nirvāṇa* with remainder because they assert that when one attains a *nirvāṇa* without remainder there is a severing of the continuum of consciousness, like the extinction of a flame. Hence, they assert that there are three final vehicles.

Some say that [according to the Vaibhāṣika system] the Teacher merely withdrew a creation of his body from the sight of some trainees when he passed from suffering [entered *parinirvāṇa*, that is, at the time of his 'death'] and did not actually pass from suffering [or completely vanish]. This is similar to a confusion of fish and turnips.

Fish and turnips are both long and white but clearly different. For this reason they are used metaphorically to indicate an absurd state of confusion.

A Buddha Superior has abandoned all sufferings and their origins without exception; and yet, it is not contradictory that true sufferings exist within his continuum. This is because the abandonment of all afflictions which take true sufferings as their objects is designated as the abandonment of true sufferings.

When all afflictions have been removed, even if one still possesses true sufferings in one's continuum, they do not give rise to afflictions, and thus it is said that all true sufferings have been abandoned.

A Buddha's physical body is included in the same lifetime as the physical base of a Bodhisattva on the path of preparation. Therefore, they assert that this body is not a Buddha Jewel [an object of refuge] although it is Buddha.

In this system a Bodhisattva is said to pass from the path of preparation to the path of no more learning in one meditative sitting; therefore, when he achieves Buddhahood, his body is the same body with which he as a Bodhisattva began the path of preparation. Since it is still an ordinary body, it cannot be an immaculate Buddha Jewel. Many scholars also say that a Buddha's body is not Buddha because it is a true suffering.

The Buddha Jewel is asserted to be the wisdom of extinction of the obstructions and the wisdom that the obstructions will never be produced again which exist in the mental continuum of a Buddha.

When one takes refuge or bows down to the Buddha Jewel, one bows not to the Buddha's body but to his wisdom. With regard to the two wisdoms, the degenerating types of Foe Destroyer attain only the wisdom of extinction of afflictions; they do not attain the wisdom of the future non-production of the afflictions.

Similarly, because Learner Superiors [those on the paths of seeing and meditation] are beings who have contamination, they are not considered to be the Community Jewel although they are the spiritual community. It is the true paths in the mental continuum of the Learner Superiors which are asserted to be the Community Jewel. There also is a presentation of the Doctrine Jewel because true cessations and *nirvāṇas* in the continuums of Hearers, Solitary Realizers, and Buddhas are all Doctrine Jewels.

A *nirvāṇa* refers to the cessation of all afflictions, whereas a true cessation is a cessation of any affliction, such as any one of the eighty-one abandonments on the path of meditation.

* * *

Thus I say:

The youthful groups with clear minds should enjoy
This feast of new ambrosia of eloquence
Taken from the ocean of the Vaibhāṣika system
With the golden vessel of my mind's analysis.

V. THE SAUTRĀNTIKAS

DEFINITION, SUBSCHOOLS AND ETYMOLOGY

The definition of a Sautrāntika is: a person propounding Hīnayāna tenets who asserts the true existence of both external objects and self-consciousness.

This definition must be qualified because it does not take into account the Sautrāntikas following scripture who do not assert self-consciousness.

'Sautrāntika' [*Sūtra*-follower] and 'Exemplifier' (*Dārṣṭāntika*) are synonyms.

There are two types of Sautrāntikas, Sautrāntikas following scripture and Sautrāntikas following reasoning. The former are [mainly] Sautrāntikas who follow Vasubandhu's *Treasury of Knowledge* and the latter are [mainly] Sautrāntikas who follow Dharmakīrti's *Seven Treatises on Valid Cognition.*

There are reasons for their being called Sautrāntikas and Exemplifiers. They are called 'Sautrāntikas' because they propound tenets chiefly in reliance on the Blessed One's *sūtras* without following the *Great Detailed Explanation.* They are called 'Exemplifiers' because they teach all doctrines by means of examples.

PRESENTATION OF THE BASIS

This section has two parts, assertions regarding objects and assertions regarding object-possessors.

Assertions regarding objects

The definition of an object (*viṣaya*) is: that which is suitable to be known by a mind. The definition of an object of knowledge (*jñeya*) is: that which is suitable to be an object of a mind. 'Object', 'existent', 'object of knowledge', and 'established base' are synonyms.

Objects are divided into the two truths; into specifically characterized objects and generally characterized objects; into negative phenomena and affirmative phenomena; into manifest phenomena and hidden phenomena; into the three times; and into the single and the different.

The two truths. The definition of an ultimate truth is: a phenomenon which is able to bear logical analysis from the point of view of whether it has its own mode of existence without depending on imputation by thought or terminology [for its existence]. 'Functioning thing', 'ultimate truth', 'specifically characterized phenomenon', 'impermanent thing', 'product', and 'truly existent phenomenon' are synonyms.

The definition of a truth for an obscured [mind] (*saṃvṛti-satya*) is: a phenomenon which only exists through being imputed by thought [or terminology]. 'Non-functioning phenomenon', 'truth for an obscured [mind]', 'generally characterized phenomenon', 'permanent [phenomenon]', 'non-product phenomenon', and 'false existent' are synonyms.

There are etymologies for the two truths. A space which is a non-product is called a truth for the obscured because it is a truth for an obscured mind. 'Obscured' here refers to a thought consciousness, which is called obscured because it is obstructed from the direct perception of specifically characterized phenomena.

A space, i.e., an absence of obstructing contact, cannot be cognized directly; it is cognized only inferentially by a conceptual or thought consciousness. A thought consciousness is said to be obscured because it cannot perceive impermanent things directly; it can perceive them only through the medium of generic images or concepts.

However, this is only an etymology [and not a definition because it is too wide]. Everything that is a truth for thought, that is, for an obscured mind, is not necessarily a truth for the obscured.

This is because a pot, for example, which is an ultimate truth, is also a truth for thought, that is, for an obscured mind. Furthermore, although a self of persons and a permanent sound are truths for thought, that is, for an obscured mind [if the mind is deluded], these do not exist even conventionally.

A pot is called an ultimate truth because it is a truth for an ultimate mind. This ultimate mind is a consciousness which is not mistaken with regard to the object appearing to it.

A thought consciousness is mistaken with respect to the object appearing to it, i.e. a generic image, because a generic image of a house, for instance, appears to be an actual house. An inferential thought consciousness, such as a consciousness that realizes the impermanence of a house, is thus mistaken only with regard to its appearing object, and not with regard to its referent object, which is the impermanence of the house and which it conceives correctly. A direct valid cognizer, however, is not mistaken with regard to either its appearing object or its referent object. Direct valid cognizers are the ultimate consciousnesses that are referred to by the word 'ultimate' in the term 'ultimate truth'.

The actual object appearing to a thought consciousness is a generic image, an image from memory, an imaginary construct, or in some cases an after-image of an object apprehended by a sense consciousness. This generic image is the same entity as the thought consciousness itself.

The *referent object* of an inferential cognizer is not a generic image of an object, but the actual object itself. For example, when one realizes the subtle impermanence of a chair, the appearing object is a generic image of an impermanent chair, and the referent object is an actual impermanent chair, but it is apprehended or referred to only indirectly, through the medium of a generic image. When one perceives the image of the horns of a rabbit, the appearing object is a generic image of the horns of a rabbit; however, the referent object, actual horns of a rabbit, does not exist. This distinction between 'appearing object' and 'referent object' is made with regard to a thought consciousness.

The generic image of fire, for instance, in a given person's mind operates in the identification of the many fires that the person perceives; therefore, that image is 'generic'. Another person would have a different image of fire, the form of which might depend on the initial identification of fire made in the present life. Thus, generic images are not general or universal in the sense that one image serves for all beings. Also, a person's generic image might change during his lifetime. Thus, a generic image is an imputation by a thought consciousness; it does not exist in and of itself and, therefore, is not a specifically characterized phenomenon and not impermanent. Though permanent, a generic image does not eternally exist, available for occasional usage by beings, nor does it exist eternally in individual minds, sometimes noticed and sometimes unnoticed. Rather, a generic image which represents the elimination of everything that is not a particular object is formed at some time and then dwells in latency until the proper conditions are assembled, such as a person's catching sight of a fire. At that time, a thought consciousness is produced with a generic image as its object which is then confused with the actual object, and the person thinks, 'This is a fire.'

Generic images are permanent, have parts, and are individual for each sentient being. They should not be confused with the permanent, partless, independent universals of other philosophical systems. The permanence of a generic image is that of occasional permanence. Another example of an occasional permanence is the space inside a pot. When the pot is destroyed, the space is no longer suitable to be designated. Also, the space inside the pot does not change moment by moment and thus cannot be called impermanent. It is an occasional permanence because it does not disintegrate momentarily as do all impermanent phenomena and also does not exist forever.

Generic images are not just images of memory which are used for the identification of objects. They are also after-images. For instance, it is said that when one actually sees an object, the object manifest before one is a specifically characterized phenomenon. An eye consciousness is produced in the image of the object, much as if a tiny mirror inside the orb of the eye were reflecting an object. The object, for example a table, exists one moment previous to the eye consciousness that is produced in its image; nevertheless, the table of the preceding moment is the object of the eye consciousness because nothing intervened between the moment of the object and the moment of the eye consciousness that apprehends the object. The specifically characterized phenomenon, table, is therefore perceived directly. If a mental consciousness is produced through the influence of that eye consciousness, the mental consciousness has one moment of direct perception of the object and thus for that moment is a mental direct perceiver. In all succeeding moments the object is an after-image.

This way of presenting the two truths is the system of the Sautrāntikas following reasoning. The Sautrāntikas following scripture assert a presentation of the two truths which accords with that of the Vaibhāṣikas.

Specifically and generally characterized objects. The definition of a specifically characterized object is: a phenomenon which is ultimately able to perform a function—for example, a pot. The definition of a generally characterized object is: a phenomenon which is ultimately unable to perform a function—for example, a space which is a non-product.

'Generality' and 'instance', 'one' and 'different', 'mutually exclusive' and 'related', and so forth, which are all imputed phenomena, are generally characterized objects; however, one should understand that an object which is any of these is not necessarily a generally characterized object.

For example, 'one' itself is a generally characterized object, but one pot is a specifically characterized object because it exists by way of its own specific nature. When we refer to a pot and say, 'It is one', that oneness is not a phenomenon which exists by way of its own specific nature because from another point of view the designation 'different' can be applied as, for example, when we refer to the pot as being different from a table. The designations 'one' and 'different' are dependent on imputation by thought; and, therefore, although they might have their base in a specifically characterized object, they themselves are generally characterized objects.

The terms *svalakṣaṇa* and *sāmānya-lakṣaṇa* which here mean 'specifically characterized object' and 'generally characterized object' are also sometimes used with a different meaning. They then refer to 'exclusive characteristic' and 'general characteristic'. An example of an exclusive characteristic is the definition of 'form'; 'impermanence' is a general characteristic of forms which is shared with other products which are not forms, such as minds.

Negative and affirmative phenomena. The definition of a negative phenomenon is: an object which is realized through the explicit elimination of an object of negation.

Because objects of knowledge are being divided into the negative and the affirmative, 'negative' here does not refer either to the act or to the object of negation. It refers to an object which is the negative, or absence, of an object of negation. For example, a negative object such as non-cow is known through eliminating cow. Non-cow includes all phenomena other than cow—house, fence, person and so forth. Although cow is not non-cow, when one says or thinks 'cow', thought does not need explicitly to eliminate non-cow.

'Negative object' and 'exclusion of the other' (*apoha*) are synonymous.

There are two types of negative phenomena, non-affirming negatives and affirming negatives. The definition of a non-affirming negative is: an object realized by a mind which explicitly realizes [that negative object] within the context of eliminating just that negative object's own negated element—for example, 'Brāhmins should not drink beer'.

This statement is a non-affirming negative because only the negated element, drinking beer, is eliminated, and nothing, no other type of food or drink for example, is affirmed in its place.

The definition of an affirming negative is: a negative which implies some other phenomenon, whether an affirmative phenomenon or another affirming negative or both, in place of its own negated element—for example, 'The fat Devadatta does not eat food during the daytime'.

In this case, the negative statement implies that Devadatta eats at night.

The definition of an affirmative phenomenon is: an object which is not realized through the explicit elimination of its own negated element by the mind actually realizing it—for example, a pot.

When thought knows or identifies a pot, it is not necessary for it explicitly to eliminate non-pot.

Manifest and hidden phenomena. The definition of a manifest phenomenon is: an object which is actually realized by a direct new valid cognizer.

In all systems except Prāsaṅgika, a valid cognizer is both new and undeceived. The second moment of a valid cognizer is no longer new, and thus is a re-cognizer, a non-new valid cognizer.

'Manifest phenomenon' and 'functioning thing' are synonyms.

From the point of view of direct cognition all functioning things are manifest phenomena.

The definition of a hidden phenomenon is: an object which is actually realized by an inferential new valid cognizer. 'Hidden phenomenon' and 'object of knowledge' are synonyms.

From the point of view of thought all objects of knowledge, including functioning things, are hidden phenomena because thought cannot perceive them directly; it can perceive them only through the medium of a generic image. Therefore, in this system 'manifest phenomenon' and 'hidden phenomenon' are not mutually exclusive. All manifest phenomena are hidden phenomena, but all hidden phenomena are not manifest phenomena; for example, a space which is a non-product can only be cognized inferentially.

The three times. The definition of a past object is: that state of having ceased which exists in the next moment after the time of an object—the object being a functioning thing that is other [than its own past].

The definition of a future object is: that state of non-production of a functioning thing which is other [than its future] in some time and place, due to the non-completion of subsidiary causes, although the main cause for its production is present.

The future of an object comes into being when that object's main cause is present but the object itself is not present; therefore, this future object exists prior to the present of that same object. For the Sautrāntikas, Cittamātrins, and Svātantrika-Mādhyamikas, past and future objects are not functioning things but are permanent, non-disintegrating. For the Prāsaṅgikas, they are functioning things and impermanent.

The definition of a present object is: that which has been produced and has not ceased.

Past and future objects are both permanent [because they are mere absences and do not undergo momentary change].

There are two types of permanence, occasional permanence and non-occasional permanence. An occasional permanence, such as the past of a table, depends on the cessation of the table, but once the cessation occurs, the past of the table which is the state of its having ceased exists unchangeably. General space, which is the lack of obstructing contact, is a non-occasional permanence; it exists forever unchangeably without a beginning.

'Prese t object' and 'functioning thing' are synonymous. These features [of past and future objects] should be known: the past of a thing occurs after that thing; the future of a thing occurs prior to that thing.

The single and the different. The definition of the single is: a phenomenon which is not diverse, such as a pot. The definition of the different is: those phenomena which are diverse, such as a pillar and a pot.

The single is what appears as single to a thought consciousness. For example, 'pot' is single; also 'pot' and 'pot' are single because the term is the same and the meaning is the same. The different are what appear to a thought consciousness to be different. 'Pillar' and 'pot' are obviously different, from the point of view of both the terms and their meanings. However, 'dog' and its Tibetan equivalent '*khyi*' are different, even though their meaning is the same because the terms themselves are different. The mention of 'dog' does not necessarily evoke '*khyi*' for a thought consciousness; therefore, the two are different, but not different entities. Similarly, product and impermanent thing are synonymous but different.

'Dog' and 'pot' are different and mutually exclusive because there is no one thing that is both a pot and a dog. However, 'dog' and 'pot' are not a dichotomy, that is, a set of two terms which include all phenomena, because if something is not a pot, it is not necessarily a dog. 'Permanent phenomenon' and 'impermanent phenomenon' are a dichotomy because, if something exists, it must be either one or the other.

'Product' and 'pot' are different, are not synonymous, are not mutually exclusive (since something can be both a product and a pot), and are not a dichotomy.

Synonyms are always the same entity, but they are different within this sameness of entity. Mutually exclusive phenomena such as a table and its colour can be the same entity but different within this sameness of entity. Mutually exclusive phenomena such as 'dog' and 'pot' are simply different entities.

Phenomena that are different entities are necessarily different opposites of the negative.

For example, 'dog' and 'pot' are different entities, and 'non-non dog' and 'non-non pot' are different because 'non-dog' and 'non-pot' are different.

However, different opposites of the negative are not necessarily different entities because 'product' and 'impermanent thing' [which are synonyms] are one entity but different opposites of the negative.

'Non-non product' and 'non-non-impermanent thing' are different because 'non-product' and 'non-impermanent thing' are different since for a thought consciousness the one term does not evoke the other.

Furthermore, they assert directionally partless atoms and temporally partless moments of consciousness in accordance with the Vaibhāṣikas.

The Vaibhāṣikas and Sautrāntikas following scripture assert these as ultimate truths because they are irreducible, whereas the Sautrāntikas following reasoning assert them as ultimate truths because they are ultimately capable of performing the function of creating effects.

However, the Sautrāntikas are not similar to the Vaibhāṣikas in all respects because the Vaibhāṣikas assert that all existents are substantially established [as having their own entity which is not dependent on thought] whereas the Sautrāntikas do not accept this. Also, both the Vaibhāṣikas and the Prāsaṅgikas assert that non-revelatory forms are actual forms, but the Sautrāntikas, Cittamātrins, and Svātantrikas do not accept these as actual forms.

Certain forms are called non-revelatory because their presence does not affect ordinary communication. An example is the subtle form of a monk's speech that is the opposite of lying and so forth but cannot be heard by others. It could, however, be heard by those with special auditory clairvoyance.

This is not the only difference between the Vaibhāṣikas and the Sautrāntikas because the Vaibhāṣikas assert some cause and effect as being simultaneous, whereas the Sautrāntikas and above do not assert this.

According to the Vaibhāṣikas, a main mind and its accompanying mental factors are simultaneously and mutually supportive, like the legs of a tripod. The Sautrāntikas and above do not assert this to be a case of simultaneous cause and effect because they maintain that the previous moment of one mental factor aids the later moment of another mental factor.

Assertions regarding object-possessors

This section has three parts, persons, consciousnesses, and terms.

Persons. The followers of scripture assert that the continuum of the five mental and physical aggregates is the person; the followers of reasoning assert that the mental consciousness is the person.

The followers of reasoning assert that the actual person is a subtle neutral type of mental consciousness because this consciousness exists continuously—through deep sleep, during meditative equipoise, and from lifetime to lifetime.

Consciousnesses. New valid consciousnesses and non-new valid consciousnesses are the two types of minds. There are two types of new valid cognizers, direct new valid cognizers and inferential new valid cognizers.

Direct new valid cognizers are of four types: sense direct perceivers, mental direct perceivers, self-consciousness direct perceivers, and yogic direct perceivers.

The followers of scripture do not accept self-consciousness.

The physical senses [such as an eye sense] are not suitable to be valid cognizers because they lack being clear consciousness and because they are incapable of knowing their objects.

There are five types of non-new valid consciousnesses: recognition, perverse consciousness, doubt, belief, and a consciousness to which an object appears without being noticed.

Re-cognition refers to the moments of direct or conceptual cognition of an object which follow the moment in which that object was newly cognized by a direct or inferential cognizer.

A perverse consciousness is any consciousness which is mistaken as to its referent object; for example, due to a fault of the eye, a perverse consciousness that perceives the moon as double is produced. A perverse consciousness should not be confused with a mistaken consciousness, which is so called because it is a consciousness that is mistaken with respect to its appearing object. The appearing object of an inferential cognizer which realizes a sound to be impermanent is a generic image of an impermanent sound; its referent object is an impermanent sound. All inferences are mistaken with regard to their appearing object because the generic image of their object appears to be the actual object. However, an inferring consciousness does not *conceive* that the generic image and the actual object are one; it does not expressly determine that 'this generic image of impermanent sound is an actual impermanent sound'. The generic image merely appears to an inferring consciousness to be an actual impermanent sound. Therefore, although an inferential consciousness is mistaken in the sense that an image appears to it to be the actual object, it is not mistaken with respect to its referent object, as in the case of understanding a sound to be impermanent. A perverse consciousness, on the other hand, is mistaken with respect to its referent object in the sense that, for instance, it sees a single moon as double.

Doubt, the third of the five non-new valid consciousnesses, is of three types. The first is doubt tending toward what is wrong, for example, a consciousness which has not decided whether a sound is permanent or not but tends toward the wrong view that a sound is permanent. The second is doubt which is equally divided between what is right and what is wrong, for example, a consciousness which tends toward both the wrong view that a sound is permanent and the right view that it is impermanent. The third is doubt tending toward what is right, such as a consciousness which has no certainty as to whether a sound is permanent or impermanent but tends toward the right view that a sound is impermanent. These three stages of doubt are often experienced successively in the process of passing from wrong views, or ignorance, to correct views, or wisdom.

Belief is a thought consciousness (not a sense consciousness) which 'decides' that, for instance, a sound is impermanent but does not have unshakeable conviction. Usually, even when many proofs demonstrating the subtle impermanence of products are given, a valid and unshakeable inference of the momentary impermanence of a sound is not immediately generated. Most persons first gain only a belief which is not entirely unshakeable and later after familiarization with correct reasoning gain an inference.

The fifth non-new valid consciousness is a consciousness to which an object appears without being noticed. This refers to a consciousness which, due to lack of interest and so forth, does not have sufficient power to draw the mental consciousness into noticing the perception. For example, when one has great interest in seeing a beautiful object, the conversation of someone close by might not be noticed. Technically, the conversation is heard, but it is not noticed and cannot be remembered.

Of these five types of non-new valid consciousnesses two, doubt and belief, are always thought consciousnesses [because they never perceive their objects directly].

When a consciousness knows its object, it realizes it within the context of having been generated in the image of its object.

Minds and mental factors are asserted to be one entity.

Terms. The definition of a term is: an object of hearing which causes the meaning that is its own object of expression to be known. If terms are divided from the point of view of their objects of expression, there are two types, terms which express types and terms which express collections. An example of the first is the term 'form'; an example of the second is the term 'pot'.

These two are not mutually exclusive. For example, the term 'pot' expresses both a type and a collection since pot is a type and is a collection composed of parts. 'Table and vase' is a term which expresses a collection but not a type.

Again, if terms are divided from the point of view of their manner of expression, there are two types: terms which express qualities and terms which express qualificands. An example of the first type is the term 'impermanence of a sound'; an example of the second type is the term 'impermanent sound'.

PRESENTATION OF PATHS

This section has three parts, objects of the paths, objects abandoned by the paths, and nature of the paths.

Objects of the paths

The sixteen aspects of the four truths, impermanence and so forth, are the objects of the paths. The Sautrāntikas assert that 'subtle selflessness' and 'subtle personal selflessness' are synonyms.

These are synonyms because the Sautrāntikas do not assert a selflessness of phenomena as do the Mahāyāna schools.

The coarse selflessness of persons is a person's emptiness of being a self that is permanent [non-disintegrating], single [partless], and independent [not depending on the mental and physical aggregates]. The subtle selflessness of persons is a person's emptiness of being substantially existent or self-sufficient [able to exist by itself].

Objects abandoned by the paths

The Sautrāntikas assert that the conception of a self is abandoned through the path. However, like the Vaibhāṣikas, they do not assert a conception of a self of phenomena, nor do they assert obstructions to omniscience. Still, they do use the terms 'afflicted ignorance' [the obstruction to liberation from cyclic existence] and 'non-afflicted ignorance' [the obstruction to the all-knowingness of a Buddha].

Nature of the paths

They make a presentation of the five paths of the three vehicles. They assert the sixteen moments of the eight paths of forbearance and the eight paths of knowledge as the path of seeing.

Because the appearing object of direct perception must be a

specifically characterized object, the Sautrrāntikas do not assert that the subtle selflessness of persons is the object of apprehension by an uninterrupted path of a Hearer's [or anyone's] path of seeing. This is because they assert that the subtle personal selflessness is realized by Hearers [and so forth] through the force of direct knowledge of products [the mental and physical aggregates] which are empty of a personal self.

The object of a non-interrupted path belonging to a path of seeing or a path of meditation must be perceived directly. Whatever is perceived directly must be a specifically characterized phenomenon, and such phenomena are always products. An emptiness, however, is a non-product and, therefore, not a specifically characterized phenomenon. Since an emptiness cannot be cognized directly, it is asserted that a yogic direct perceiver does not directly cognize selflessness. Rather, it cognizes the mind and body as no longer qualified with such a self. Thus, it is products, the mental and physical aggregates, which are directly cognized, and thereby the emptiness of a personal self is implicitly realized. This fact greatly distinguishes the Sautrāntikas from the Mahāyāna schools which assert direct cognition of emptiness itself.

PRESENTATION OF THE FRUITS OF THE PATHS

The Sautrāntikas assert that there is no Foe Destroyer who falls from his abandonment [of all afflictions] or from his realization [of the subtle personal selflessness]. They also assert that the form aggregate of a Buddha is a Buddha. Other than this, the Sautrāntikas' assertions on the ways of manifesting the fruits of the three vehicles and so forth are similar to those of the Vaibhāṣikas.

Both the Vaibhāṣikas and the Sautrāntikas maintain that the scriptural divisions of the Mahāyāna [discipline (*vinaya*), sets of discourses (*sūtrānta*), and knowledge (*abhidharma*)] are not the word of Buddha. However, it is said that later Vaibhāṣikas and Sautrāntikas do assert them to be the word of Buddha.

* * *

Thus I say:

Those propounding reason should take delight
In this expression of the secret words of logic
Of the Exemplifiers following reason, accurate
From my good training in the books of logic.

VI. THE CITTAMĀTRINS

DEFINITION, SUBSCHOOLS AND ETYMOLOGY

The definition of a Cittamātrin is: a person propounding Buddhist tenets who asserts the true existence of dependent phenomena but does not assert external objects.

Cittamātrins are of two types, true aspect Cittamātrins and false aspect Cittamātrins. Differences exist between these two groups; an appearance of a blue [patch] as blue to an eye consciousness perceiving blue is the 'aspect' that is the basis of debate between the true and false aspectarians.

The true aspectarians assert that an appearance of blue as blue to an eye consciousness perceiving blue exists as it appears.

They hold that a blue patch which appears as a gross or coalesced object does in fact exist as a gross or coalesced object in the manner in which it appears, whereas the false aspectarians say it does not. Being Cittamātrins, the true aspectarians agree with the false aspectarians that the appearance of a blue patch as an external object is false. However, unlike the false aspectarians, the true aspectarians maintain that within the context of this false appearance the portion of the appearance as a gross object is correct.

The false aspectarians maintain that an appearance of blue as blue does not exist as it appears to an eye consciousness which perceives blue [because the sense of grossness exceeds what is actually there].

The above presentation is correct because both the true and false aspectarians are similar in asserting that blue appears as blue to an eye consciousness which perceives blue.

This means that both accept that there are eye consciousnesses which perceive blue as blue and not as yellow, for there are objects which are the same entity as a perceiving consciousness even though there is no external world. Similarly, both agree that there are eye consciousnesses which perceive blue as yellow, due to some fault in the eye.

They are also similar in asserting that blue [falsely] appears to be an external object.

Both true and false aspectarians agree that even to valid sense consciousnesses objects appear falsely as if they were entities external to the perceiving consciousness.

The true aspectarians assert that an appearance of blue as an external object to an eye consciousness perceiving blue is polluted by ignorance, but that an appearance of blue as blue and an appearance of blue as a gross object is not polluted by ignorance.

The false aspectarians assert not only that an appearance of blue as an external object is polluted by ignorance, but also that an appearance of blue as a gross object is polluted by ignorance.

Therefore, the definition of a true aspect Cittamātrin is: a Cittamātrin who asserts that an appearance of a gross object to a sense consciousness exists as it appears. The definition of a false aspect Cittamātrin is: a Cittamātrin who asserts that an appearance of a gross object to a sense consciousness does not exist as it appears.

There are three types of true aspect Cittamātrins: proponents of an equal number of objects and subjects, half-eggists, and non-pluralists.

Only in the Cittamātra and Yogācāra-Svātantrika systems do object and subject exist simultaneously. One latency (*vāsanā*) or seed (*bīja*) simultaneously produces both object and subject. For instance, one latency would produce the mottle of colours on the wing of a butterfly as well as producing the eye consciousness which apprehends these colours. The object is said to 'appear toward' the perceiving subject. Thus, there is a question of whether just one aspect of the object, the mottle, appears to the subject, or whether many aspects of the object, such as the blue, yellow, red, and so forth, appear to the subject. Also, every school except the Vaibhāṣika asserts that the perceiving subject, such as an eye consciousness, comes to be like its object, much as a mirror comes to be like an object set before it. Thus, a similar question is asked: does an eye consciousness come to be produced in the many aspects of the object, an aspect of red, an aspect of blue, an aspect of yellow, and so forth? Or, more simply, the question is this: at any one moment are there many eye consciousnesses which perceive the individual aspects of the object or is there one eye consciousness which perceives the object in general?

If there are many eye consciousnesses each moment, it would seem to contradict scripture which says that a plurality of consciousnesses of similar type does not occur at the same moment, even though an eye consciousness, an ear consciousness, a nose consciousness, a tongue consciousness, a body consciousness, and a mental consciousness may exist at the same moment. On the other hand, if there is only one eye consciousness every moment, then how are all the individual aspects of the object perceived?

A few possible 'solutions' are:

(1) there are many eye consciousnesses each moment equal in number to the number of aspects belonging to the object;

(2) there is one general eye consciousness which apprehends the mottle, and there are many parts of that eye consciousness which individually apprehend the individual colours;

(3) there is only one eye consciousness each moment, and moment by moment the various aspects are serially apprehended.

All three of these are represented in the Sautrāntika system where an external world is asserted. The Cittamātrins offer another set of three which are given below.

It is important to determine just what 'aspect' (*ākāra, rnam pa*) is being discussed in a passage, for there are many meanings to this word. In general, *viṣaya-ākāra* (*yul rnam*) means the object itself; *grahya-ākāra* (*gzung rnam*) means the perceiving subject; *grahaka-ākāra* (*'dzin rnam*) means the perceiver of the perceiving subject, that is, self-consciousness. However, sometimes *grahya-ākāra* (*gzung rnam*) refers to the object rather than the subject.

Drung-chen Lek-pa-sang-po [Drung-chen Legs-pa-bzang-po], Panchen So-nam-drak-pa [Panchen bSod-nams-grags-pa], and so forth interpret the three types of true aspectarians as follows.[13] Proponents of an equal number of subjects and objects assert that just as the blue and the yellow, which appear to a sense consciousness apprehending a mottle, are different entities, the eye consciousnesses depending on the eye consciousness apprehending the mottle are different entities. Half-eggists assert that though in general a [patch of] blue and an eye consciousness apprehending that blue are of the nature of the mind, they are different entities.

They are called half-eggists because they are one half like the Sautrāntikas and one half like the Cittamātrins.

The non-pluralists assert that just as the blue and yellow of a mottle are one entity, so the sense consciousnesses which apprehend the blue and the yellow and which depend on the eye consciousness apprehending the mottle are one entity.

Proponents of an equal number of objects and subjects are of two types: those who assert eight consciousnesses [the five sense consciousnesses, a mental consciousness, an afflicted mind (*kliṣṭa-manaḥ*), and a mind basis of all (*ālaya-vijñāna*)]; and those who assert six consciousnesses.

Non-pluralists are said to be of two types, proponents of six consciousnesses and proponents of a single consciousness.

It is said that the false aspectarians are of two types, tainted false aspectarians and non-tainted false aspectarians. Tainted false aspectarians are so called because they assert that the nature of the mind is tainted by the latencies of ignorance. Non-tainted false aspectarians are so called because they assert that mind is not in the least tainted by the latencies of ignorance.

Or, according to another interpretation, the tainted false aspectarians are so called because they assert that although there is no ignorance at the stage of Buddhahood, there are mistaken appearances. Also, non-tainted false aspectarians are so called because they assert that because there is no ignorance at the stage of Buddhahood, there are also no mistaken appearances.

Jang-kya rejects both interpretations of tainted false aspectarians saying that there is no Buddhist system which asserts that the nature of the mind itself is polluted or that a Buddha has false perception.[14]

Further, Cittamātrins can be divided into two types: followers of scripture and followers of reasoning. The former are followers of Asaṅga's *Five Treatises on the Levels*, and the latter are followers of Dharmakīrti's *Seven Treatises on Valid Cognition.*

They are called Cittamātrins and Vijñaptivādins because they propound that all phenomena are of the entity of the mind. Further, because they settle the practice of the deeds of the path from the yogic point of view, they are also called Yogācārins.

PRESENTATION OF THE BASIS

This section has two parts, assertions regarding objects and assertions regarding object-possessors.

Assertions regarding objects

The Cittamātrins assert that all objects of knowledge are included in the three natures.

These three are dependent phenomena (*paratantra*) [literally other-powered phenomena], thoroughly established phenomena (*pariniṣ-panna*), and imaginary phenomena (*parikalpita*).

This is so because they assert that all products are dependent phenomena, that the natures of all phenomena [emptinesses] are thoroughly established phenomena, and that all other objects of knowledge are imaginaries.

Except for emptinesses, all permanent phenomena such as spaces are imaginaries. All emptinesses are thoroughly established phenomena. All impermanent phenomena are dependent phenomena. In this way, all phenomena are included within the three natures.

Imaginaries are of two types, existent and non-existent. All permanent objects of knowledge, except for emptinesses, are included in the category of existent imaginaries. Non-existent imaginaries are not objects of knowledge, and thus they are not phenomena. For example, a permanent self or a table which is a separate entity from the consciousness perceiving it do not exist at all; these are non-existent imaginaries.

They assert that the three natures exist in their own right and exist inherently.

If a class has both existent and non-existent members, the class itself is considered to be existent. Thus, imaginaries in general are existent even though some imaginaries, such as a permanent self, do not exist. Therefore, as a class, even imaginaries exist inherently.

However, there are differences with regard to whether the natures truly exist or not, because the Cittamātrins assert that imaginaries do not truly exist and that both dependent phenomena and thoroughly established phenomena truly exist.

The definition of an imaginary is: that which does not ultimately exist but exists for thought. Imaginaries are of two types, existent imaginaries and non-existent imaginaries. An example of an existent imaginary is 'object of knowledge'.

As generalities, 'object of knowledge', 'one', 'different', and so forth are permanent because their instances are both permanent and impermanent. In determining the classification of a category, existence predominates over non-existence and permanence predominates over impermanence.

Examples of non-existent imaginaries are the two selves.

The two selves are a self of persons and a self of phenomena. Persons are empty of being substantial or self-sufficient entities, and phenomena are empty of being subjects and objects which are different entities. Thus, a non-existent imaginary is something which exists for thought, such as a substantially existent person, but which does not actually exist at all. Existent imaginaries, on the other hand, do actually exist but only in dependence on thought, as in the case of a space which can only be realized through eliminating obstructing contact.

The definition of a dependent phenomenon is: that which arises in dependence on the power of others, that is, causes and conditions, and which is a base of a thoroughly established phenomenon [an emptiness].

All products are dependent phenomena because they arise in dependence on the causes which produce them. A dependent phenomenon is a base of a thoroughly established phenomenon because it is empty of being a separate entity from a consciousness that perceives it. Thus every product is the base of this quality of emptiness.

There are two types of dependent phenomena, pure and impure.

Pure dependent phenomena are, for example, the wisdom of Superiors subsequent to meditative equipoise and the major and minor marks of a Buddha.

A Superior (one who has attained a path of seeing) directly cognizes emptiness during meditative equipoise. His wisdom at that time is a pure dependent phenomenon. When he rises from meditation, he has a second type of wisdom; this is the knowledge that although subject and object appear to be different entities, they are not different entities. This knowledge is indirect or conceptual whereas during meditative equipoise he had direct cognition of emptiness.

Impure dependent phenomena are, for example, the mental and physical aggregates which are appropriated [through contaminated actions and afflictions].

The definition of a thoroughly established phenomenon is: a suchness which is an emptiness of either of the two selves [a self of persons or of phenomena]. There are two types of thoroughly established phenomena, non-perverse and immutable. An example of the first is a Superior's wisdom during meditative equipoise. An example of the second is the final nature of a phenomenon.

Although non-perverse thoroughly established phenomena are said to be a division of thoroughly established phenomena, they actually are not thoroughly established phenomena. This is so because they are not final objects of awareness of a path of purification by which obstructions are removed.

A Superior's wisdom is not an emptiness because it is a consciousness; it is a cognizer of emptiness in the mode of being fused with emptiness. The two are fused like fresh water in fresh water, but they are nevertheless different for thought. Therefore, it cannot be said that this wisdom itself is an emptiness, and thus it cannot serve as an object of meditation which would remove obstructions.

Further, there are two types of objects of knowledge, conventional truths and ultimate truths. The definition of a conventional truth is: an object found by a valid cognizer which is a correct knower that distinguishes a conventionality. 'Falsity', 'nominal truth', and 'conventional truth' are synonyms.

All objects except emptinesses are falsities because they do not exist the way they appear, that is, as separate entities from a perceiver. However, in this system, impermanent phenomena and emptinesses truly exist, because the Cittamātrins maintain that if these phenomena exist, they necessarily truly exist.

The definition of an ultimate truth is: an object found by a valid cognizer which is a correct knower that distinguishes an ultimate. 'Emptiness', 'element of [superior] qualities' (*dharmadhātu*), 'thoroughly established phenomenon', 'ultimate truth', 'limit of reality', and 'suchness' are asserted to be synonyms.

Ultimate truths necessarily exist by way of their own nature, but conventional truths do not necessarily exist by way of their own nature. This is because dependent phenomena exist by way of their own nature, but imaginary phenomena [which are also conventional truths] do not exist by way of their own nature [although they inherently exist and exist in their own right].

Existent imaginaries, such as spaces, are conventional truths, but non-existent imaginaries, such as a permanent self or a table which is a separate entity from a perceiving consciousness, are not even conventional truths because they do not exist.

Falsities do not necessarily falsely exist, for although dependent phenomena are falsities, they do not falsely exist.

In the Cittamātra system dependent phenomena are falsities, but they do not falsely exist. This is because, if they did not truly exist, they would not exist at all. They are false in the sense that due to the subject's own predispositions they appear to exist as entities separate from a perceiving consciousness. The fact that they truly exist prevents the extreme of non-existence. Their falseness in the sense of appearing one way but existing another prevents the extreme of existence.

Sautrāntikas, Cittamātrins and Svātantrikas all agree in their presentations of the three times and of non-affirming negatives.

These three schools assert that past and future objects are permanent phenomena, that is, mere absences, and that present objects are impermanent. They, along with the Prāsaṅgikas, agree that negatives do not necessarily imply something in their place.

The five sense objects, forms and so forth, do not exist as external objects because they are produced within the entity of an internal consciousness through the power of seeds established by particular actions on the mind basis of all (*ālaya-vijñāna*).

The true aspectarians assert that the five sense objects, forms and so forth, are not external objects but do exist as gross objects. The false aspectarians maintain that, if such were the case, then forms and so forth would have to be external objects; therefore, they assert that the five types of sense objects do not exist as gross objects [although they do, of course, accept part and whole].

Assertions regarding object-possessors

The followers of scripture [mainly the followers of Asaṅga] assert eight consciousnesses; therefore, they assert that the mind basis of all is the person. The followers of reasoning [mainly the followers of Dharmakīrti] assert that the mental consciousness is the person.

This does not mean that all mental consciousnesses are the person, for there are many types of mental consciousnesses, desire, hatred, and so on. The mental consciousness that is the actual person is a subtle, neutral form of the mental consciousness which exists unceasingly throughout the whole life. It is called the mental consciousness which is the base of the name of the person. It is much like the mind basis of all but is not separated off as a different entity from the other forms of the mental consciousness.

The followers of scripture assert that a mind basis of all apprehends [the five senses, the five objects, and] the internal latencies.

The actual objects of awareness of a mind basis of all are the five senses and the five types of objects which are apprehended by the five sense consciousnesses. It is not actually aware of the latencies, but it is said to be aware of them because all perceptions are produced by the latencies.

A mind basis of all has the aspect of not discriminating its objects [it does not identify, 'This is such and such'] and its entity is undefiled and neutral. It is a constant main mind, associated only with the five omnipresent mental factors. Moreover, from among the two possibilities of being defiled or non-defiled, it is non-defiled and neutral.

It is non-defiled because it is not accompanied by afflicted mental factors. The five omnipresent mental factors are contact, feeling, discrimination, intention, and mental activity.

A mind basis of all is not virtuous because it exists in the continuum of one whose roots of virtue are severed. It is also not non-virtuous because those of the upper realms have a mind basis of all; [therefore, it is neutral].

In the form and formless realms, even the mental factors of pride and so forth are not non-virtuous but neutral.

The object of awareness of an afflicted mind (*kliṣṭa-manaḥ*) is a mind basis of all.

However, it does not perceive the actual entity of a mind basis of all as it is, for if it did, it would not perceive it as a self-sufficient person.

Its aspect is that of considering the mind basis of all to be [a substantially existent or self-sufficient] 'I'. Its entity is defiled and neutral.

An afflicted mind has nine accompanying mental factors, the five omnipresent mental factors and four mental factors which defile it: attachment to self, obscuration about self, pride in self, and view of self. When these four defiling mental factors are cleared away, the entity of an afflicted mind still exists, but it is then pure. At Buddhahood an afflicted mind is transformed into a wisdom of equality which views all objects equally as not different entities from the consciousness perceiving them.

In general, their way of presenting the six consciousnesses agrees with the common Buddhist presentation of the six consciousnesses.

[Both followers of scripture and followers of reasoning] assert that valid cognizers are of two types, direct and inferential, and they also assert a presentation of four types of direct valid cognizers. Self-consciousness direct perceivers and yogic direct perceivers are necessarily non-mistaken consciousnesses.

True aspectarians assert that even an eye consciousness in the continuum of the short-sighted [an ordinary being] that perceives blue is a non-mistaken consciousness with respect to the portion of the appearance of blue as blue.

Etymologically, the term 'short-sighted' or 'one who looks near-by' refers to one who does not see beyond ordinary worldly appearances.

According to the false aspectarians, all sense direct perceivers in the continuum of the short-sighted are necessarily mistaken consciousnesses. Also, they assert that mental direct perceivers in such a continuum are of two types, mistaken and non-mistaken.

Many other scholars assert that all instances of both sense direct perceivers and mental direct perceivers in the continuum of an ordinary being are mistaken because objects appear to them to be separate entities from the perceiving consciousness.

PRESENTATION OF PATHS

This section has three parts, objects of the paths, objects abandoned by the paths, and the nature of the paths.

Objects of the paths

The sixteen aspects of the four noble truths are impermanence and so forth. The coarse selflessness of persons is a person's emptiness of being permanent, partless, and independent. The subtle selflessness of persons is a person's emptiness of being substantially existent or self-sufficient.

There are two subtle selflessnesses of phenomena. One is a form and its valid cognizer's emptiness of being separate entities; the other is a form's emptiness of naturally being the base of apprehension for a thought consciousness which conceives of form.

A form is not a separate entity from a consciousness apprehending it, and a consciousness of a form is not a separate entity from its object. Also, forms, consciousnesses, and so forth are not naturally bases of the affixing of their respective names.

Both subtle selflessnesses [of persons and of phenomena] are asserted to be emptinesses. However, an emptiness is not necessarily either of these, for both true cessations and *nirvāṇas* are accepted as emptinesses.

This is a technical point. A true cessation is an emptiness in the continuum of one who has utterly extinguished an obstruction, and it must be either of the two selflessnesses. But once it can be either, in general it is neither.

A product is asserted to be the same substantial entity (*dravya*) as the valid cognizer that apprehends it. A phenomenon that is a non-product is asserted to be the same entity (*vastu*) as the valid cognizer that apprehends it.

Objects abandoned by the paths

The objects abandoned by the paths are the afflictive obstructions (*kleśāvaraṇa*) and the obstructions to [simultaneous cognition of all] objects of knowledge (*jñeyāvaraṇa*).

These may be translated less literally as obstructions to liberation and obstructions to omniscience.

The obstructions to liberation are, for instance, the conception of a coarse or subtle self of persons, together with their seeds, as well as the six main afflictions and twenty secondary afflictions.

The six main afflictions are desire, hatred, ignorance, pride, wrong view, and doubt. The twenty secondary afflictions are anger, enmity, resentment, harmfulness, jealousy, dishonesty, dissimulation, non-embarrassment, non-shame, concealment, miserliness, haughtiness, non-faith, laziness, non-conscientiousness, forgetfulness, non-introspection, dullness, excitement, and distraction.

The obstructions to omniscience are, for instance, the conceptions of a self of phenomena, together with their latencies.

Bodhisattvas take the obstructions to omniscience as their main object of abandonment; they do not take the obstructions to liberation as their main object of abandonment. Hīnayāna trainees [Hearers and Solitary Realizers] take the obstructions to liberation as their main object of abandonment and do not take the obstructions to omniscience as their main object of abandonment.

Nature of the paths

A presentation of the five paths—the paths of accumulation, preparation, seeing, meditation, and no more learning—is made for each of the three vehicles. The Cittamātrins also assert a presentation of the ten Bodhisattva grounds for the Mahāyāna.

The first of the ten grounds begins with the path of seeing which is also the beginning of the Superior's path. The remaining nine grounds are the path of meditation.

PRESENTATION OF THE FRUITS OF THE PATHS

Those whose lineage is definite as that of the Hīnayāna take as their main object of meditation a thoroughly established phenomenon which is a selflessness of persons. When familiarity with this object is complete, then in dependence on the *vajra*-like meditative stabilization of the Hīnayāna path of meditation, they abandon all the obstructions to liberation and simultaneously actualize the fruit of a Hīnayāna Foe Destroyer.

There is not even the slightest difference between Hearers and Solitary Realizers regarding the selflessness which is their object of meditation, or regarding the afflictions which are their objects of abandonment. Therefore, the presentation of the eight Enterers and Abiders applies to both. However, Solitary Realizers only live in the desire realm [and do not exist in the form or formless realms]; therefore, the arrangement of the twenty members of the spiritual community does not apply to them.

Still, it is not the case that there are no differences at all between Hearers and Solitary Realizers. It is asserted that Hearers are inferior and Solitary Realizers are superior from the point of view that a Solitary Realizer amasses the collections of merit for one hundred aeons, whereas a Hearer does not. The fruits that arise for Solitary Realizers and Hearers in accordance with these practices are respectively superior and inferior.

The Cittamātra followers of scripture do not assert that a Hīnayāna Foe Destroyer who merely goes to peace ever enters the path of the Mahāyāna. However, they assert that a Foe

Destroyer whose enlightenment becomes transformed [into that of a Bodhisattva] enters the path of the Mahāyāna. This entry is from a *nirvāṇa* with remainder. There is no entry from a *nirvāṇa* without remainder because they assert that there are three final vehicles.

A remainderless *nirvāṇa* is asserted to be a severance of the continuum of form and consciousness, like the extinguishing of a lamp. Thus, it would be impossible to enter the Mahāyāna at that point.

The Cittamātra followers of reasoning assert that all Hīnayāna Foe Destroyers enter into the Mahāyāna because they assert that there is only one final vehicle.

Those who have the Mahāyāna lineage take as their main object of meditation a thoroughly established phenomenon which is a selflessness of phenomena. They practise meditation on the selflessness of phenomena in conjunction with [amassing] the collections of merit over three countless aeons and step by step traverse the five paths and the ten grounds. By means of the uninterrupted path at the end of their continuum [as a sentient being who still has obstructions to be abandoned] they completely abandon the two obstructions, thereby attaining Buddhahood in a Highest Pure Land. They attain a Truth Body, the abandonment of obstructions and realization of selflessness which is the perfection of their own welfare, and attain the two Form Bodies [Complete Enjoyment Body and Emanation Body], the perfection of activities for others' welfare.

According to some followers of Asaṅga's *Compendium of Knowledge* (*Abhidharma-samuccaya*), it appears that complete enlightenment also can occur in a human life.

They maintain that Buddhahood can be attained in a human body, not just with the special body of one in a Highest Pure Land.

Regarding the word of Buddha, Cittamātrins accept the distinction of definitive scriptures and scriptures requiring interpretation. For they assert that the first two wheels of doctrine as presented in the *Unravelling of the Thought Sūtra* are scriptures requiring interpretation and that the final wheel is comprised of definitive scriptures. They designate a scripture whose explicit teaching cannot be accepted literally as a *sūtra* requiring interpretation. They designate any scripture whose explicit teaching can be accepted literally as definitive.

There are three types of *nirvāṇas*: with remainder, without remainder, and non-abiding (see pp. 128, 130).

There are Three Bodies of a Buddha, Truth Body (*Dharmakāya*), Complete Enjoyment Body (*Saṃbhogakāya*), and Emanation Body (*Nirmāṇakāya*). A Truth Body is of two types, a Nature Body and a Wisdom Body. Also, there are two Nature Bodies, a naturally pure Nature Body and a Nature Body as freedom from the adventitious defilements.

A Wisdom Body is a Buddha's omniscient consciousness, and a Nature Body is the emptiness of a Buddha's omniscient consciousness. In the sense that a Buddha's mind has always been essentially free of the defilements, the emptiness of his mind is called a naturally pure Nature Body. In the sense that a Buddha's mind has become free of the adventitious defilements, the emptiness of his mind is called a Nature Body as freedom from the adventitious defilements.

Because they assert all of these, the Cittamātrins are called proponents of Mahāyāna tenets.

* * *

Thus I say:

It is right for the discriminating to enter here with joy
To the tenets of those propounding mind-only
Who follow the word of the Subduer, the Leader,
Since this was stated true to the word of many sages.

VII. THE MĀDHYAMIKAS: 1. THE SVĀTANTRIKAS

DEFINITION, SUBSCHOOLS AND ETYMOLOGY OF MĀDHYAMIKA

A Mādhyamika is a person propounding Buddhist tenets who asserts that there are no truly existent phenomena, not even particles.

There are two types of Mādhyamikas: Svātantrika-Mādhyamikas and Prāsaṅgika-Mādhyamikas.

They are called Mādhyamikas because they assert a middle way which is free from the extremes of permanence and annihilation. They are called proponents of no entityness (*niḥsvabhāvavādin*) because they propound that phenomena have no entityness (*niḥsvabhāvatā*), that is, no true existence.

Svabhāva has three usages: (1) the conventionally existent nature of a phenomenon, such as the heat of fire; (2) the real or final nature of a phenomenon, that is, its emptiness or non-true existence; (3) true or independent existence. All Mādhyamikas assert the existence of the first and second and refute the third.

This chapter deals in detail with the Svātantrikas; the Prāsaṅgikas are the subject of Chapter VIII.

THE SVĀTANTRIKAS: DEFINITION, ETYMOLOGY AND SUBSCHOOLS

A Svātantrika is a person who propounds no entityness and who asserts that phenomena exist by their own nature conventionally [although not ultimately].

They are called Svātantrika-Mādhyamikas because they refute true existence through relying on a correct logical mark whose three aspects exist objectively.

A correct logical mark (*liṅga*) or reason (*hetu*) must have three qualities: the mark must be a quality of the subject; the mark must be pervaded by the predicate, i.e. the predicate must be something that is always true of the reason; and the opposite of the predicate must be pervaded by the opposite of the mark. For example, in the syllogism, 'A person does not truly exist because of being a dependent-arising', 'person' is the subject, 'non-truly existent' is the predicate, and 'dependent-arising' is the mark or reason. The reason is a quality of the subject because a person is a dependent-arising. The predicate pervades the reason because all dependent-arisings do not truly or independently exist. There is a counterpervasion because hypothetically all non-dependent-arisings would be truly existent. The Svātantrikas assert that a correct reason inherently or naturally possesses these three aspects within the context of not ultimately existing. This means that they do not have a mode of existence which is not posited through appearing to the mind.

There are two divisions, Yogācāra-Svātantrika-Mādhyamika and Sautrāntika-Svātantrika-Mādhyamika.

The definition of a Yogācāra-Svātantrika-Mādhyamika is: a Mādhyamika who asserts self-consciousness and does not assert external objects. An example is the teacher Śāntirakṣita.

The definition of a Sautrāntika-Svātantrika-Mādhyamika is: a Mādhyamika who does not assert self-consciousness and who asserts that external objects exist by way of their own nature. An example is the teacher Bhāvaviveka.

There are also etymologies for Yogācāra-Svātantrika and Sautrāntika-Svātantrika. The former are called Yogācāra-Svātantrikas because they assert a presentation of objects in accordance with the Yogācārins, and the latter are called Sautrāntika-Svātantrikas because, like the Sautrāntikas, they assert external objects to be aggregates of particles.

Yogācāra-Svātantrikas are of two types, those who accord with true aspectarians and those who accord with false aspectarians. Examples of the first are Śāntirakṣita, Kamalaśīla, and Ārya

Vimuktisena. Examples of the second are the teachers Haribhadra, Jetāri, and Lāvapa. Jetāri accords with the tainted false aspectarians, and Lāvapa accords with the non-tainted false aspectarians.

In the following pages the tenets of the two subschools are presented separately: (*a*) the system of the Yogācāra-Svātantrika-Mādhyamikas; (*b*) the system of the Sautrāntika-Svātantrika-Mādhyamikas.

TENETS OF THE YOGĀCĀRA-SVĀTANTRIKA-MĀDHYAMIKAS

PRESENTATION OF THE BASIS

This section has two parts, assertions regarding objects and assertions regarding object-possessors.

Assertions regarding objects

An object necessarily exists by way of its own nature, because they assert that, regarding any phenomenon, if the imputed object is sought, it is findable. Therefore they assert that 'inherently existent' (*svabhāva-siddha*), 'existing by way of its own nature' (*svalakṣaṇa-siddha*), 'existing by way of its own mode of subsistence', and 'existing in its own right' (*svarūpa-siddha*) are synonymous.

There are two types of objects of knowledge, ultimate truths and conventional truths. The definition of an ultimate truth is: an object which is non-dualistically realized by a direct valid cognizer that actually cognizes it.

When an ultimate truth, an emptiness, is cognized, it is realized in an utterly non-dualistic manner without any appearance of subject and object, and it is only an ultimate truth which can be non-dualistically cognized.

The definition of a conventional truth is: an object which is dualistically realized by a direct valid cognizer that actually cognizes it.

'Duality' here refers to an appearance of subject and object which in this system are conventionally one entity.

An example of an ultimate truth is a pot's emptiness of true existence. An example of a conventional truth is a pot.

If an extensive division of ultimate truths is made, there are sixteen [or twenty] emptinesses. Or, in brief, there are four emptinesses.

The four emptinesses are of products, non-products, self, and other.

There are two types of conventional truths, real conventional truths and unreal conventional truths. An example of the first is water; an example of the second is a mirage.

A mirage exists but is commonly known to be unreal because it appears to be water but is not.

In this system a consciousness is necessarily a real conventionality.

Assertions regarding object-possessors

Both Yogācāra-Svātantrikas and Sautrāntika-Svātantrikas assert that [a subtle, neutral] mental consciousness is the [actual] person. They do not assert a mind basis of all or an afflicted mind but assert six consciousnesses.

There are two kinds of minds, new valid consciousnesses and non-new valid consciousnesses. There are two types of new valid cognizers, direct new valid cognizers and inferential new valid cognizers.

[For the Yogācāra-Svātantrikas] there are four types of direct new valid cognizers: sense direct perceivers, mental direct perceivers, self-consciousness direct perceivers, and yogic direct perceivers. They assert that all instances of self-consciousness and yogic direct perceivers are unmistaken consciousnesses.

These are not mistaken either with respect to the non-difference of entity of subject and object or with respect to non-true existence.

A direct perceiver apprehending a blue [patch] and the blue [patch] itself are asserted to be one entity because they do not accept external objects.

PRESENTATION OF PATHS

This section has three parts, objects of the paths, objects abandoned by the paths, and nature of the paths.

Objects of the paths

The Yogācāra-Svātantrikas assert that a person's emptiness of being a permanent, partless, independent self is a coarse selflessness of persons. They assert that a person's emptiness of being a substantially existent or self-sufficient self is a subtle selflessness of persons.

The coarse selflessness of persons is also applicable to phenomena in the sense that all phenomena are empty of being objects of use of a permanent, partless, independent user. The subtle selflessness of persons also applies to phenomena in that all phenomena are empty of being objects that are used by a substantially existent or self-sufficient user. Thereby it is seen that according to the Svātantrikas the base of the emptiness of persons is not just the person but all phenomena. Further, the bases of the emptiness of phenomena are not just phenomena (excluding the person) but also the person. Thus the bases of the two emptinesses are the same; however, the object negated in, for instance, the subtle selflessness of persons is substantial existence whereas the object negated in the subtle selflessness of phenomena is true existence. Thus, for the Svātantrikas the bases of the emptiness of a self of persons and the bases of the emptiness of a self of phenomena are the same, but the object negated, or that of which the bases are empty, is different. 'Base of emptiness' here means an object that is empty of a negated element and should not be misunderstood as a physical base out of which phenomena are produced. Still, it can be said that emptiness is the base of all phenomena because if phenomena were not empty of true existence, they could not be produced or destroyed.

The Yogācāra-Svātantrikas assert that a form's emptiness of being an entity other than a valid cognizer apprehending the form is a coarse selflessness of phenomena. They assert that the emptiness of true existence in all phenomena is the subtle selflessness of phenomena.

Objects abandoned by the paths

The Yogācāra-Svātantrikas assert that the conceptions of a self of persons are the obstructions to liberation. They assert that the conceptions of a self of phenomena are the obstructions to omniscience.

There are two types of obstructions to omniscience. The conception of an otherness of entity of subject and object is the coarse obstruction to omniscience, and the conception of the true existence of phenomena, such as the mental and physical aggregates, is asserted to be the subtle obstruction to omniscience.

Nature of the paths

The Yogācāra-Svātantrikas assert the five paths of the three vehicles, making fifteen paths, just as the other systems do. The difference is in their assertion that an uninterrupted path and a path of liberation of a Solitary Realizer must have the aspect of realizing an emptiness of duality [of subject and object].

Each level of the path has a path of liberation that is the experience of having vanquished the obstructions which must be abandoned before that level is achieved. Each level also has an uninterrupted path which is the meditative equipoise vanquishing the obstructions of that level. It leads directly, without interruption, to the attainment of the next path of liberation, which is the beginning of the next level, during the same meditative equipoise.

'Emptiness of duality' here refers to subject and object's emptiness of being different entities. The aspect of a path is its mode of apprehension. A path is a consciousness which when actualized will lead one to high attainments.

PRESENTATION OF THE FRUITS OF THE PATHS

Solitary Realizers take as their main object of abandonment the coarse obstruction to omniscience [the conception that subject and object are different entities]. Therefore, the presentation of the eight Enterers and Abiders is not applicable to Solitary Realizers.

Because a Solitary Realizer strives mainly to abandon the coarse obstructions to omniscience, the eight Enterers and Abiders which deal with abandoning the obstructions to liberation do not apply to him.

However, the eight Enterers and Abiders are asserted with respect to Hearers.

Those firm in the Hearer lineage take as their main object of cultivation the view realizing the selflessness of persons. Finally, in dependence on the *vajra*-like meditative stabilization of their path of meditation, they abandon all obstructions to liberation and simultaneously actualize the fruit of Hearer Foe Destroyer.

Those firm in the Solitary Realizer lineage take as their main object of cultivation the view that subject and object are empty of being different entities. Finally, in dependence on the *vajra*-like meditative stabilization of their path of meditation, they abandon all obstructions to liberation as well as all the coarse obstructions to omniscience and simultaneously attain the fruit of Solitary Realizer Foe Destroyer.

Hīnayāna *nirvāṇas* are of two types, those with remainder and those without. The first is a *nirvāṇa* having the remainder of [miserable] mental and physical aggregates which were wrought by former actions and afflictions. The second type is asserted to be a state free of [miserable] mental and physical aggregates. A Hearer or Solitary Realizer Foe Destroyer will necessarily enter the Mahāyāna vehicle because they assert only one final vehicle.

Thus in this system, due to a difference in the objects of abandonment and in the type of realization of Hearers and Solitary Realizers, there is also a distinction of inferiority and superiority with respect to the fruits which they attain.

Those firm in the Mahāyāna lineage generate an altruistic aspiration to highest enlightenment. Then, during the Mahāyāna path of accumulation, in dependence on the meditative stabilization of the stream of doctrine they actually listen to teachings from superior Emanation Bodies. When, in dependence on their practising the meaning of these instructions, they first attain the wisdom which arises from meditation directed toward emptiness, they pass on to the path of preparation.

Then at the time of heat [the first of four levels in the path of preparation], the manifest conception of thoroughly afflicted objects [as truly existent objects of use] diminishes. At the time of attaining peak [the second step of the path of preparation], the manifest conception of pure objects [such as true cessations and true paths as truly existent objects of use] diminishes. When endurance [the third step of the path of preparation] is attained, the manifest conception [of a truly existent user] with regard to a subject which apprehends objects as real diminishes. When 'highest mundane qualities' [the fourth and last step of the path of preparation] is attained, the manifest conception [of a truly existent user] with regard to a subject which apprehends objects as imputed diminishes. These four conceptions are abandoned on the path of seeing.

The four, heat, peak, endurance, and highest mundane qualities, are respectively called the meditative stablization of achieving perception [of emptiness], the meditative stablization of the increase of the perception [of emptiness], the meditative stablization which understands suchness one-sidedly, and the uninterrupted meditative stabilization.

The meditative stabilization which understands suchness one-sidedly is so called because for the first time a yogī has attained clear conceptual perception of the emptiness of objects but he has not yet understood the emptiness of subjects; thus, his concentration is one-sided with respect to emptiness. The uninterrupted concentration is so called because in the same session the yogī will pass on without interruption to a path of liberation which is the beginning of the path of seeing.

After that, all the artificial obstructions to liberation and the artificial obstructions to omniscience together with their seeds are removed by an uninterrupted path of the path of seeing. A path of liberation [of the path of seeing] and a true cessation [of the artificial obstructions] are then actualized.[15]

Artificial obstructions to liberation refer to superimpositions of a self of persons that are not inborn but intellectually acquired. Conviction in self is gained through teachings and proofs of, for instance, a self-sufficient person. Artificial obstructions to omniscience refer to superimpositions of a self of phenomena which derive from conviction gained through the teachings and proofs of a difference of entity of subject and object or of true existence.

The path of liberation here is the experience of having vanquished the artificial obstructions. True cessation here is the state of cessation, completely and forever, of the artificial obstructions.

Through the nine steps of the path of meditation the seeds of the sixteen afflictions and the seeds of the one hundred and eight obstructions to omniscience which are to be abandoned by the path of meditation are gradually abandoned. Finally, in dependence on the uninterrupted path at the end of the continuum [of existence as a sentient being] the innate afflictions and the innate obstructions to omniscience are simultaneously abandoned. In the next moment highest enlightenment is attained.

Upon the attainment of Buddhahood one is no longer a 'sentient being' (*sattva*), but this does not mean that a Buddha has no mind. Because a Buddha has no mind which has obstructions yet to be abandoned, he is not a 'sentient being', a term which is applicable only to one with obstructions yet to be abandoned. The innate obstructions are the conceptions of a self of persons and a self of phenomena which derive from the beginningless habit of viewing persons and phenomena as, for instance, truly existent. The term 'innate' or 'inborn' means that these obstructions are produced along with the mental and physical aggregates without the need of conviction gained through teachings and proofs.

This is the way the fruit is manifested by those who are firm in the Bodhisattva lineage.

They assert that Mahāyāna *nirvāṇa* and non-abiding *nirvāṇa* are synonymous.

In a non-abiding *nirvāṇa* there is no abiding in cyclic existence due to wisdom, and there is no abiding in solitary peace due to compassion.

They assert that there are definitely Four Bodies of a Buddha. Even though Ārya Vimuktiṡena and Haribhadra debated about the teachings regarding the Bodies of a Buddha [in Maitreya's *Ornament to the Realizations*], they did not debate about the number.

The Four Bodies of a Buddha are Nature Body, Wisdom Body, Complete Enjoyment Body, and Emanation Body.

The word of Buddha is divided into definitive scriptures and scriptures requiring interpretation. Scriptures requiring interpretation are those which either are not suitable to be asserted literally or whose main object of explication is the actual teaching of conventional truths. A definitive scripture is a scripture suitable to be asserted literally that actually teaches ultimate truths as its main object of explication.

For a scripture to be definitive it must be literally acceptable, without qualification. For instance, even a passage teaching that all phenomena are empty of inherent existence requires interpretation; though the main object taught is an ultimate truth, the passage cannot be accepted without the qualification 'ultimately' (*paramārthataḥ*), that is, all phenomena are ultimately empty of inherent existence.

With respect to the wheels of doctrine as explained in the *Unravelling of the Thought Sūtra*, the first wheel requires interpretation; the last two wheels are both asserted to have two types, definitive and requiring interpretation.

TENETS OF THE SAUTRĀNTIKA-SVĀTANTRIKA-MĀDHYAMIKAS

PRESENTATION OF THE BASIS

Except that this system asserts external objects and does not assert self-consciousness, it mostly resembles the Yogācāra-Svātantrika-Mādhyamika.

PRESENTATION OF PATHS

The Sautrāntika-Svātantrika-Mādhyamikas assert that those firm in the lineage of Hearers and Solitary Realizers do not realize the selflessness of phenomena. Also, they do not assert a wisdom which realizes that subject and object are empty of being different entities, and they do not assert that the conception of external objects is an obstruction to omniscience.

PRESENTATION OF THE FRUITS OF THE PATHS

The obstructions which Hearers and Solitary Realizers abandon and the selflessness which they realize do not differ in coarseness or subtlety. Thus, there is no difference in their type of realization. The Sautrāntika-Svātantrikas make a presentation of the eight Enterers and Abiders for both Hearers and Solitary Realizers.

They assert that those firm in the Mahāyāna lineage abandon the two obstructions serially. For, Bhāvaviveka explains in his *Blaze of Reasoning* (*Tarkajvālā*) that at the time of achieving the eighth ground the obstructions to liberation are exhaustively abandoned. However, unlike the Prāsaṅgikas, they do not assert that one begins to abandon the obstructions to omniscience only when the obstructions to liberation have all been removed.

The Sautrāntika-Svātantrikas say that Bodhisattvas on the first ground simultaneously begin to rid themselves of the obstructions to liberation and the obstructions to omniscience but that the final removal of the two obstructions does not take place simultaneously. The completion of the abandoning of the obstructions to liberation takes place at the beginning of the eighth Bodhisattva ground, and the completion of the abandoning of the obstructions to omniscience takes place at Buddhahood.

Except for these differences, the Sautrāntika-Svātantrikas' presentation of the basis, paths, and fruits mostly accords with that of the Yogācāra-Svātantrika-Mādhyamikas.

* * *

Thus I say:

> Those who wish to be wise, take up this exposition
> Expressing well, without fabrication, all the varieties
> In tenets of the Svātantrikas asserting
> That things, though naturally existent, do not truly exist.

VIII. THE MĀDHYAMIKAS: 2. THE PRĀSAṄGIKAS

DEFINITION AND ETYMOLOGY

The definition of a Prāsaṅgika is: a proponent of no entityness who does not assert that phenomena exist by way of their own nature even conventionally. Examples are Buddhapālita, Candrakīrti, and Śāntideva.

Why are they called Prāsaṅgikas? They are called Prāsaṅgikas [those who use consequences] because they assert that an inferring consciousness which realizes the thesis [that phenomena do not inherently exist] can be generated in the continuum of an opponent just by [presenting him with an absurd] consequence [of his own position].

The Prāsaṅgikas say that the consequence, 'It follows that the person is not a dependent-arising because of inherently existing', can generate in another the understanding that a person does not inherently exist because of being a dependent-arising. The other systems hold that, after presenting a consequence, it is necessary to state its import in syllogistic form in order to cause an opponent to realize the intended thesis.

PRESENTATION OF THE BASIS

They assert that no objects exist by way of their own nature. This is because they assert that all objects are only imputed by thought and that the word 'only' in the term 'only imputed by thought' eliminates natural existence. 'Established base', 'object', and 'object of knowledge' are synonyms.

Assertions regarding objects

Objects are divided into the manifest and the hidden, and they are divided into the two truths.

The manifest and the hidden. The definition of a manifest object is: a phenomenon which can be known through the power of experience, without depending on a logical mark. 'Directly knowable', 'manifest object', 'sense object', and 'non-hidden phenomenon' are synonyms. Examples are forms, sounds, odours, tastes, and tangible objects.

The definition of a hidden object is: a phenomenon which must be known through depending on a reason or mark. 'Hidden object', 'non-manifest phenomenon', and 'object of inferential comprehension' are synonyms. Examples are the impermanence of a sound and the non-inherent existence of a sound.[16]

These definitions are taken from the point of view of ordinary beings because there are no hidden objects for a Buddha, who realizes everything directly. Also, an ordinary being who has a yogic direct perceiver which directly realizes the subtle impermanence of, for instance, a sound must depend on infernece before directly cognizing it. A Superior, however, can directly perceive the impermanence of a sound without first dpending on an inference. Thus the impermanence of a sound is not always a hidden object; it can be perceived directly as under the above conditions. Consequently, the synonyms given are only rough synonyms because what is an object of inference for one person could be an object of direct perception even for another ordinary being. The point here is that a hidden object is something which an ordinary being can *newly* cognize *only* through inference.

Therefore, in this system a manifest object and a hidden object are mutually exclusive [for ordinary beings]. Also, the three spheres of objects of comprehension [the manifest, the slightly hidden, and the very hidden] are asserted to be mutually exclusive.

Slightly hidden objects, such as an emptiness of inherent existence, are amenable to realization by the usual type of inference. The very hidden, such as the layout of the universe, are known through such means as valid scriptures.

The two truths. The definition of a conventional truth is: an object which is found by a valid cognizer distinguishing a conventionality and with respect to which a valid cognizer distinguishing a conventionality becomes a valid cognizer distinguishing a conventionality. An example is a pot.

A sufficient definition of a conventional truth which applies to anyone but a Buddha is: an object found by a valid cognizer which distinguishes a conventionality, that is, any existent except an emptiness. A Buddha's single consciousness distinguishes both conventionalities (everything except emptinesses) as well as final phenomena (emptinesses). Thus, a Buddha is said to have a valid cognizer which distinguishes conventional phenomena from the point of view of the object only, as in the case of a pot. Similarly, a Buddha is said to have a valid cognizer which distinguishes final phenomena only from the point of view of the object, as in the case of the emptiness of a pot. Thus, with respect to different objects a Buddha is said to have valid cognizers which distinguish conventional phenomena and which distinguish final phenomena. However, a Buddha's valid cognizer which distinguishes conventional phenomena actually also distinguishes final phenomena, and a Buddha's valid cognizer which distinguishes final phenomena also distinguishes conventional phenomena. Therefore, with respect to a Buddha, an object found by a valid cognizer which distinguishes conventional phenomena is not necessarily a conventional phenomenon. Similarly, with respect to a Buddha, an object found by a valid cognizer which distinguishes final phenomena is not necessarily a final phenomenon. The second part of the definition, therefore, is given for the sake of including the objects of a Buddha's cognitions within the framework of the definition.

Conventional truths are not divided into real conventionalities and unreal conventionalities. This is because there are no real conventionalities, for conventionalities are necessarily not real because conventionalities are necessarily unreal [in the sense that they are not findable under analysis]. However, with reference to a common worldly consciousness conventional truths are divided into the real and the unreal. For with reference to a common worldly consciousness a body is real, and with reference to a common worldly consciousness a face reflected in a mirror is unreal. Still, whatever is real with reference to a common worldly consciousness is not necessarily existent; truly existent forms are real with reference to a common worldly consciousness [but are totally non-existent].

The definition of an ultimate truth is: an object found by a valid cognizer distinguishing a final phenomenon [an emptiness] and with respect to which a valid cognizer distinguishing a final phenomenon becomes a valid cognizer distinguishing a final phenomenon. An example is a pot's non-inherent existence. The divisions of ultimate truths are as given above [p. 124].

Furthermore, past objects, future objects, and states of cessation are asserted to be functioning things [capable of producing an effect, rather than permanent phenomena as the Sautrāntikas, Cittamātrins, and Svātantrikas assert]. Also, the Prāsaṅgikas assert external objects because they assert that object and subject are different entities.

Assertions regarding object-possessors

The Prāsaṅgikas assert that a person is the mere 'I' that is imputed in dependence on its bases of imputation, which are either the five mental and physical aggregates [in the desire and form realms] or the four aggregates [in the formless realm].

In the Prāsaṅgika system a person is the dependently imputed 'I', not the mental consciousness, nor the composite of aggregates, nor a mind basis of all as the other systems say.

All persons are necessarily compositional factors that are neither form nor consciousness.

A person is not any of his bases of designation and shares the qualities of all the mental and physical aggregates. Therefore, persons are included in the fourth aggregate among non-associated compositional factors. Thus, though a person is technically an instance of the fourth aggregate, a person is still not any of the aggregates which serve as his basis of designation.

Consciousnesses are of two types, valid and non-valid. Valid consciousnesses are of two types, direct valid cognizers and inferential valid cognizers. Direct valid cognizers are of three types, sense direct perceivers, mental direct perceivers, and yogic direct perceivers. The Prāsaṅgikas do not accept self-consciousness.

All sense consciousnesses in the mental continuum of a sentient being are necessarily mistaken.

Sense consciousnesses of sentient beings are mistaken in that objects appear to them to exist inherently. This type of mistake is limited to 'sentient beings', those who have minds with obstructions yet to be removed. Thus, the term 'sentient being' includes all conscious beings except Buddhas. Only sense consciousnesses of sentient beings are said to be mistaken because Bodhisattvas in meditative equipoise on emptiness perceive emptiness directly with their mental consciousness in a non-mistaken manner. They are sentient beings because they have obstructions yet to be removed, and their mental consciousness at the time of directly cognizing emptiness is totally non-mistaken. Therefore, not all consciousnesses but all sense consciousnesses of sentient beings are mistaken. Also, when Bodhisattvas (or Hearers or Solitary Realizers) rise from meditative equipoise on emptiness, their sense and mental consciousnesses again come under the influence of previously acquired predispositions which cause objects to appear as if inherently existent.

Yogic direct perceivers are of two types, mistaken and non-mistaken. A yogic direct perceiver that is in non-contaminated meditative equipoise [on emptiness] is non-mistaken, and a yogic direct perceiver of a common person that directly realizes subtle impermanence is a mistaken consciousness.

The latter is mistaken because impermanence appears to it to be inherently existent. Subtle impermanence is the moment by moment disintegration of products and is difficult to realize. Examples of coarse impermanence are death, the breaking of an object, and so on, which can be realized very easily.

It follows that a yogic direct perceiver of a common person is a mistaken consciousness because it is a consciousness in the mental continuum of a common person.

All sense and mental consciousnesses of common persons are mistaken whereas with regard to sentient beings (a term that includes Superiors) only the sense consciousnesses are mistaken because a mental consciousness directly cognizing emptiness in the continuum of a Superior is non-mistaken. Conversely, all consciousnesses of a Buddha are non-mistaken. This means that a Buddha's consciousness—sense consciousness or mental consciousness—neither perceives nor conceives objects as being inherently existent whether in or out of meditative equipoise.

All re-cognizers are necessarily direct valid cognizers. The second moment of an inferring consciousness which realizes that a sound is impermanent is a conceptual direct valid cognizer. Also, the second moment of a sense direct perceiver apprehending a form is a non-conceptual direct valid cognizer.

In the Prāsaṅgika system *pramāṇa* (valid cognizer) does not refer to a cognizer which *newly* realizes its object in such a manner that its cognition is incontrovertible. Rather, *pramāṇa* refers just to a valid, right, or incontrovertible cognizer which is not mistaken with respect to its referent object; it is not necessarily perceiving its object for the first time. Thus for the Prāsaṅgikas a valid cognizer yields incontrovertible knowledge with respect to its main object, but it is not necessarily new as the other systems maintain.

To understand what the other systems mean by 'new', consider the following. Often because of intense concentration on an object one does not notice other objects which nevertheless are 'perceived'. For instance, when watching a particularly interesting object of sight, one might not notice what was said within hearing range. The ear consciousness heard the sound, but what was heard was not noticed by the mental consciousness at that time, nor could it be remembered in the future. Such a consciousness is not a *pramāṇa* because although the object appeared to it clearly, no notice was taken of what was perceived. Thus, even though one might be in contact with an object for some time, one might not notice the object due to lack of attention. Also, a consciousness of an ordinary being cannot apprehend a single instant of an object. Whether attention is intense or not, it takes many instants before an ordinary being can notice an object.

If the object of a consciousness is not noticed, that consciousness is not a *pramāṇa*. For a consciousness to be a *pramāṇa*, there must be a noticing of the object. Thus, according to the non-Prāsaṅgika use of the term, a 'sense direct valid cognizer' refers to a correct sense consciousness for that period of time required to notice an object initially. The subsequent moments of consciousness in the same continuum of attention to that object, during which no other noticed perceptions intervene, are called re-cognizers. This is because in those moments an object which was formerly noticed is being cognized again. In all systems except Prāsaṅgika, a re-cognizer is not a *pramāṇa* because it does not newly realize its object. However, the Prāsaṅgikas do not gloss the *pra* of *pramāṇa* as 'first' or 'new'; they gloss it as 'valid', 'right', or 'main'; and thus, for them a re-cognizer is a *pramāṇa*, a valid cognizer.

The same holds true for an inferential consciousness. Once an inference has been produced, its subsequent moments are re-cognizers which the Prāsaṅgika system alone accepts as *prāmaṇa*, valid cognizers. Since the subsequent moments of an inferential consciousness do not rely again on a reason in order to cognize the object, the second period is no longer inferential but direct. This is because it remembers the object already inferred *directly*, that is, without renewed reliance on a logical reason. Therefore, in the Prāsaṅgika system, unlike the other systems, a direct perceiver can be conceptual. A re-cognizer of an already inferred object which does not rely again on a logical mark in its cognition is a conceptual direct perceiver. Even though direct, it nevertheless is conceptual because it cognizes its referent object through the medium of an image. 'Direct' here means not relying on a logical mark.

A re-cognizer which is the subsequent moment of a direct sense perceiver is a non-conceptual direct valid cognizer.

Inference is of four types: inference by the power of evidence [that serves as a logical mark such as the presence of dependent-arising which is a sign of non-inherent existence]; inference by renown [such as coming to know that the sound 'moon' is suitable to express that object]; inference through example [such as inferring what a cow without a dewlap is through knowledge of a cow with a dewlap]; and inference through correct belief [in scriptures which are not implicitly or explicitly contradicted by other scriptures, inference, or direct perception].

Being mistaken with respect to an object and realizing that object are not mutually exclusive, because the Prāsaṅgikas assert that an inferential cognizer which realizes that a sound is impermanent is mistaken with respect to [the inherent existence of] impermanent sound [although it does correctly realize the impermanence of a sound].

'Mistaken' here refers to the appearance of what does not inherently exist as inherently existent. Thus a consciousness may correctly ascertain an object but may be mistaken in that the object appears to it to be inherently existent.

Dualistic consciousnesses are necessarily direct valid cognizers with respect to their own appearing object. This is because even a conceptual consciousness which misconceives sound to be permanent is a direct valid cognizer with respect to its appearing object.

Its appearing object is merely a generic image of permanent sound and not actual permanent sound because permanent sound does not exist. The consciousness is valid *with respect to its appearing object* because it notices and can induce memory of this generic image, no matter how erroneous it is.

A conceptual consciousness which conceives sound to be permanent is not itself a valid cognizer because it is not a correct knower. However, if one considers merely the appearance of its object, which is an idea or image of permanent sound, then it is valid with respect to this appearance because validity involves a noticing of the object and an ability to remember it. Thus, even a perverse consciousness is a valid cognizer with respect to its own appearing object.

All consciousnesses [correct, perverse, conceptual, or non-conceptual] cognize their own objects of comprehension. For, a generic image of the horns of a rabbit is the object of comprehension of a conceptual consciousness apprehending the horns of a rabbit; and a generic image of permanent sound is the object of comprehension of a conceptual consciousness apprehending permanent sound.

PRESENTATION OF PATHS

Objects of the paths

The coarse selflessness of persons is asserted to be a person's emptiness of substantial existence or self-sufficiency. Also, the subtle emptiness of persons is asserted to be a person's emptiness of true existence.

The two subtle selflessnesses [of persons and of phenomena] are differentiated from the point of view of the bases which are predicated by emptiness [persons and phenomena]. They are not differentiated from the point of view of the object of negation. This is because true existence is the object of negation, and a negative of true existence in relation to a person—a base of negation—is a subtle selflessness of persons. Also, a negative of true existence—the object of negation—in relation to a mental or physical aggregate or the like—a base of negation—is a subtle selflessness of phenomena. A subtle selflessness of persons and a subtle selflessness of phenomena are asserted to be equally subtle and to be the final mode of existence [of persons and other phenomena].

Objects abandoned by the paths

The coarse and subtle conceptions of a self, together with their seeds, and the three poisons which arise through their influence, together with their seeds, are asserted to be the obstructions to liberation. This is so because the Prāsaṅgikas assert that the conception of true existence is an obstruction to liberation. The latencies of the conception of true existence, the mistaken appearances of [inherently existent] duality which arise through their influence, and the taints of apprehending the two truths as different entities are asserted to be the obstructions to omniscience.

The seeds of the conception of true existence produce the *conception* that phenomena and persons truly exist, but the latencies of the conception of true existence produce an *appearance* of persons and phenomena as inherently existent.

Nature of the paths

The Prāsaṅgikas present the five paths for each of the three vehicles. Also, relying on the *Sūtra on the Ten Grounds* (*Daśabhūmika*) they presen tthe ten grounds for the Mahāyāna. The three vehicles do not have different types of wisdom because the Prāsaṅgikas assert that all Superiors directly cognize the selflessness of phenomena.

PRESENTATION OF THE FRUITS OF THE PATHS

Those firm in the Hīnayāna lineage cultivate the view of selflessness merely through brief reasoning. In dependence on this they finally remove the conception of true existence, together with its seeds, through the *vajra*-like meditative stabilization of the Hīnayāna path of meditation and simultaneously actualize the Hīnayāna enlightenment.

The Svātantrika-Mādhyamikas and below assert that in order to attain a *nirvāṇa* without remainder it is first necessary to attain a *nirvāṇa* with remainder. However, in the Prāsaṅgika system it is asserted that prior to a *nirvāṇa* with remainder it is necessary to attain a *nirvāṇa* without remainder.

The Prāsaṅgikas have a different meaning for the two terms. For them, a *nirvāṇa* without remainder refers to the meditative equipoise on emptiness during which a Hīnayānist finally becomes a Foe Destroyer. At that time he has overcome the conception of inherent existence and thus possesses a *nirvāṇa*, a passing beyond sorrow, with 'sorrow' identified as the obstructions to liberation. Since at that time he is directly cognizing emptiness, he also is temporarily free of the appearance of inherent existence and thus is said not to have any 'remainder' of this false appearance. However, when he rises from equipoise, things appear to exist inherently even though he never again will assent to this false appearance and thereby conceive things to exist inherently. Thus, a Foe Destroyer first has a *nirvāṇa* without remainder and then a *nirvāṇa* with remainder. Gradually, a Foe Destroyer enters the Mahāyāna and after a great accumulation of merit also purifies his perception of the false appearance of inherent existence. He thereby eliminates the obstructions to omniscience and becomes a Buddha.

The Prāsaṅgikas assert a presentation of the eight Enterers and Abiders for Hearers and Solitary Realizers, and they assert that all Enterers and Abiders are Superiors.

The way the Mahāyāna enlightenment is actualized is this:

Bodhisattvas extensively cultivate the view of selflessness through innumerable forms of reasoning and thereby remove the obstructions. Until the obstructions to liberation are exhaustively abandoned, they do not begin to abandon the obstructions to omniscience. They begin to abandon the obstructions to omniscience on the eighth Bodhisattva ground which is when Bodhisattvas who did not initially go on a Hīnayāna path exhaustively abandon the obstructions to liberation. Finally, through depending on the non-interrupted path at the end of the continuum [of being a sentient being] they abandon, without residue, all obstructions to omniscience and simultaneously actualize the state of the Four Buddha Bodies.

The Prāsaṅgikas assert that all *nirvāṇas* and true cessations are ultimate truths.

A *nirvāṇa* is an emptiness of the mind in the continuum of one who has completely and forever abandoned all afflictions. A true cessation is an emptiness of the mind in the continuum of one who has completely and forever abandoned a portion of the afflictions.

The first and last of the three wheels of doctrine as explained in the *Unravelling of the Thought Sūtra* are scriptures that require interpretation because they do not contain any passages which explicitly teach emptiness.

This refers only to the three wheels *as set forth* in the *Unravelling of the Thought Sūtra*. According to the Prāsaṅgikas' own way of setting forth the three wheels of doctrine, certain passages in the first and third wheels are also definitive because they teach emptiness, the final nature of phenomena, explicitly.

They assert that the middle wheel of doctrine is composed of definitive scriptures because the *Heart Sūtra* (*Prajñāpāramitā-hṛdaya*) is a definitive scripture.

The main distinguishing feature of Prāsaṅgika is that based on the reason that internal and external phenomena are dependently imputed, they refute that phenomena exist by way of their own nature. However, within their own system and without needing to rely on [the ignorance of] others they know how to establish without fault bondage and liberation, cause and effect, known and knower and so forth, conventionally, only nominally, that is, as only imputedly existent. Nowadays, some who are vain about having high views say that phenomena are only mistaken appearances and take them to be utterly non-existent, like the son of a barren woman; then they hold that non-attention to anything is the superior practice. They do not even have the scent of Prāsaṅgika in them.

Therefore, those who seek liberation, having seen all the marvels of cyclic existence as being like a whirlwind of fire, should abandon all bad views which are fabricated to look like doctrine and should strive toward the Mādhyamika-Prāsaṅgikas' own system, the highest of all systems of tenets.

* * *

Thus I say:

The depth of the terms and meanings gathered on the golden earth
Of the systems of doctrine is difficult to fathom.
Successive waves of various reasonings move about,
Causing fear in the hearts of children of low intellect.

Splitting into a thousand rivers of manifold views,
It is a place of sport for birds of clear intellect.
Who can measure all the particulars of the great
Treasure of water of outer and inner systems of doctrine?

However, the boat obtained by a being,
Impelled by a favourable wind bringing fortune,
Goes to the centre of the ocean of tenets
And presently finds this jewelled garland of eloquence.

The youthful groups of those with clear intellect
Wishing to spread the feast of eloquent song
Before millions of the best of the wise should rely
On this brief explanation of our own and others' tenets.

O, the wonder of those nowadays vainly considering themselves
To be wise, running off from the top of their heads, without training
A long time in the great books, assuming the tiring task
Of the dance of composition for the sake of wealth and respect!

Thousands of rays of eloquence from the sky of analysis
Shine forth and close all the faulty explanations[17]
But cause to smile the white countenance of the marvellous meanings
Of the great forest with hundreds of petals of the correct systems.

This book clarifying countless tenets containing the essence
From the books of Indian and Tibetan scholars
Was not done through competitiveness or jealousy but for the sake
Of furthering the intellect of those whose lot is similar to mine.

Through this good deed arising from effort,
Suppressing with its brilliance even the light of the moon
May all beings be freed from the chasm of bad views
And may the correct path sustain them forever.

Thus, this brief presentation of outer and inner tenets called *A Precious Garland* was composed by the reverend Kön-chok-jik-may-wang-po (dKon-mchog-'jigs-med-dbang-po) during the waxing of the sixth month in the water-snake year. He composed it in the face of requests by the faithful, energetic, and discriminating Nga-wang-kal-sang (Ngag-dbang-skal-bzang) and the monk Nga-wang-sang-po (Ngag-dbang-bzang-po). His secretary was Ta-drin-tse-ring (rTa-mgrin-tshe-ring).

May this translation into English bring a measure of help and happiness to sentient beings.

GLOSSARY

ENGLISH	SANSKRIT	TIBETAN
action	*karma*	*las*
activity	*rajaḥ*	*rtul*
afflicted mind	*kliṣṭa-manaḥ*	*nyon yid*
aggregates	*skandha*	*phung po*
Analyser	*Mīmāṃsaka*	*dPyod pa ba*
anus	*pāyu*	*rkub*
arms	*pāṇi*	*lag pa*
body	*sparśana*	*pags pa/lus*
commentaries (on Buddha's Word)	*śāstra*	*bstan bcos*
community	*saṃgha*	*tshogs*
Complete Enjoyment Body	*Saṃbhoga-kāya*	*Longs sku*
compositional factor not associated with either mind or mental factors	*citta-caitta-viprayukta-saṃskāra*	*sems sems byung dang ldan par ma yin pa'i 'du byed*
conventional truth	*saṃvṛti-satya*	*kun rdzob bden ba*
cyclic existence	*saṃsāra*	*'khor ba*
darkness	*tamaḥ*	*mun pa*
dependent phenomenon	*paratantra*	*gzhan dbang*
desire realm	*kāma-dhātu*	*'dod khams*
direct valid cognizer/ direct new valid cognizer	*pratyakṣa-pramāṇa*	*mngon sum tshad ma*
discipline	*vinaya*	*'dul ba*
doctrine	*dharma*	*chos*
ear	*śrota*	*rna*
earth	*pṛthvī*	*sa*
element of [superior] qualities	*dharmadhātu*	*chos dbyings*
Emanation Body	*Nirmāṇakāya*	*sPrul sku*
entity	*vastu*	*ngo bo*

ENGLISH	SANSKRIT	TIBETAN
entity/substantial entity	*dravya*	*rdzas*
entityness	*svabhāvatā*	*ngo bo nyid*
Enumerator	*Sāṃkhya*	*Grangs can pa*
exclusion of the other	*apoha*	*gzhan sel*
Exemplifier	*Dārṣṭāntika*	*dPe ston ba*
exist validly	*pramāṇa-siddha*	*tshad mas grub pa*
existent	*sat*	*yod pa*
existing by way of its own mode of subsistence	?	*rang gi sdod lugs gyi ngos nas grub pa*
existing by way of its own nature	*svalakṣaṇa-siddha*	*rang gi mtshan nyid kyis grub pa*
existing in its own right	*svarūpa-siddha*	*rang ngos nas grub pa*
eye	*cakṣuḥ*	*mig*
fire	*tejaḥ*	*me*
Foe Destroyer	*Arhan*	*dGra bcom pa*
Forder	*Tīrthika*	*Mu stegs pa*
form	*rūpa*	*gzugs*
Form Body	*Rūpa-kāya*	*gZugs sku*
form realm	*rūpa-dhātu*	*gzugs khams*
formless realm	*ārūpya-dhātu*	*gzugs med khams*
fundamental nature	*prakṛti*	*rang bzhin*
generally characterized phenomenon/object	*sāmānya-lakṣaṇa*	*spyi mtshan*
generic image	*artha-sāmānya*	*don spyi*
genitalia	*upastha*	*'doms*
great one	*mahat*	*chen po*
ground	*bhūmi*	*sa*
Hearer	*Śrāvaka*	*Nyan thos*
Hedonist	*Cārvāka/Ayata*	*rGyang 'phen pa*
Highest Pure Land	*Akaniṣṭa*	*'Og min*
imaginary	*parikalpita*	*kun btags*
inherently existent	*svabhāva-siddha*	*rang bzhin gyis grub pa*
intellect	*buddhi*	*blo*
intellectual faculty	*manaḥ*	*yid*
I-principle	*ahaṃkāra*	*nga rgyal*
Jewel Superior Rarity	*Ratna*	*dKon mchog*
knowledge	*abhidharma*	*chos mngon pa*

ENGLISH	SANSKRIT	TIBETAN
latency	*vāsanā*	*bag chags*
leg	*pāda*	*rkang pa*
lightness	*sattva*	*snying stobs*
logical mark	*liṅga*	*rtags*
Logician	*Naiyāyika*	*Rigs pa can*
main mind	*citta*	*sems*
meditative stabilization	*samādhi*	*ting nge 'dzin*
mental and physical aggregates	*skandha*	*phung po*
mental factor	*caitta*	*sems byung*
mind basis of all	*ālaya-vijñāna*	*kun gzhi rnam shes*
Nature Body	*Svabhāvika-kāya*	*Ngo bo nyid sku*
new valid cognizer	*pramāṇa*	*tshad ma*
no entityness	*niḥsvabhāvatā*	*ngo bo nyid med pa*
non-associated compositional factor	*viprayukta-saṃskāra*	*ldan min 'du byed*
non-product	*asaṃskṛta*	*'dus ma byas*
non-thing	*abhāva*	*dngos med*
non-valid consciousness	*apramāṇa-buddhi*	*tshad min gyi blo*
nose	*ghrāṇa*	*sna*
object	*viṣaya*	*yul*
object aspect	*viṣaya-ākāra*	*yul rnam*
object of knowledge	*jñeya*	*shes bya*
obstruction to liberation/ obstructions which are the afflictions	*kleśāvaraṇa*	*nyon sgrib*
obstruction to omniscience/ obstruction to simultaneous cognition of all phenomena	*jñeyāvaraṇa*	*shes sgrib*
obtainer	*prāpti*	*thob pa*
odour	*gandha*	*dri*
Particularist	*Vaiśeṣika*	*Bye brag pa*
path of accumulation	*saṃbhāra-mārga*	*tshogs lam*
path of meditation	*bhāvanā-mārga*	*sgom lam*
path of no more learning	*aśaikṣa-mārga*	*mi slob lam*
path of preparation	*prayoga-mārga*	*sbyor lam*
path of seeing	*darśana-mārga*	*mthong lam*
perceiver of the perceiving subject aspect	*grahaka-ākāra*	*'dzin rnam*

ENGLISH	SANSKRIT	TIBETAN
perceiving subject aspect	*grahya-ākāra*	*gzung rnam*
person	*puruṣa*	*skyes bu*
principle	*pradhāna*	*gtso bo*
proponent of no entityness	*niḥsvabhāvavādin*	*ngo bo nyid med par smra ba*
reason	*hetu*	*gtan tshigs*
reliquary	*stūpa*	*mchod rten*
Ritualist/Analyser	*Mīmāṃsaka*	*dPyod pa ba*
seed	*bīja*	*sa bon*
self	*ātman*	*bdag*
self-consciousness	*svasaṃvedanā*	*rang rig*
selflessness of persons	*pudgala-nairātmya*	*gang zag gi bdag med*
selflessness of phenomena	*dharma-nairātmya*	*chos kyi bdag med*
sentient being	*sattva*	*sems can*
sets of discourses	*sūtrānta*	*mdo sde*
Solitary Realizer	*Pratyekabuddha*	*Rang sangs rgyas*
sound	*śabda*	*sgra*
space	*ākāśa*	*nam mkha'*
special insight	*vipaśyanā*	*lhag mthong*
specifically characterized phenomenon/object	*svalakṣaṇa*	*rang mtshan*
speech	*vāc*	*ngag*
Spiritual Community	*Saṃgha*	*dGe 'dun*
substantially established	*dravya-siddha*	*rdzas grub*
substantially existent	*dravya-sat*	*rdzas yod*
Superior	*Ārya*	*'Phags pa*
Sūtra Follower	*Sautrāntika*	*mDo sde pa*
tangible object	*spraṣṭavya*	*reg bya*
taste	*rasa*	*ro*
tenet/established conclusion	*siddhānta*	*grub mtha'*
thing/functioning thing	*bhāva*	*dngos po*
thoroughly established phenomenon	*pariniṣpanna*	*yongs grub*
thought	*vikalpa*	*rtog pa*
tongue	*rasana*	*lce*
Truth Body	*Dharma-kāya*	*Chos sku*
truth for a concealer	*saṃvṛti-satya*	*kun rdzob bden pa*
truth for an obscured mind	*saṃvṛti-satya*	*kun rdzob bden pa*

ENGLISH	SANSKRIT	TIBETAN
ultimate truth	*paramārtha-satya*	*don dam bden pa*
ultimately	*paramārthataḥ*	*don dam par*
valid cognizer	*pramāṇa*	*tshad ma*
valid consciousness	*pramāṇa-buddhi*	*tshad ma'i blo*
water	*āp*	*chu*
wind	*vāyu*	*rlung*
Wisdom Truth Body	*Jñāna-dharma-kāya*	*Ye shes chos sku*
Word of Buddha	*Buddhavacana*	*bka'*

NOTES

PART ONE: PRACTICE

1. The text wrongly read: 'There are three [parts], thought on the difficulty of finding precious leisure and fortune, thought that the time of death is indefinite, and thought of the sufferings in bad migrations.'

PART TWO: THEORY

1. Jam-yang-shay-ba ('Jam-dbyangs-bzhad-pa), *An Explanation of 'Tenets', A Sun of the Land of Samantabhadra Brilliantly Illuminating All of Our Own and Others' Tenets and the Meaning of the Profound Emptiness, An Ocean of Scripture and Reasoning Fulfilling All Hopes of All Beings* (*Grub mtha'i rnam bshad rang gzhan grub mtha' kun dang zab don mchog tu gsal ba kun bzang zhing gi nyi ma lung rigs rgya mtsho skye dgu'i re ba kun skong*) [known as the *Great Exposition of Tenets* (*Grub mtha' chen mo*) and hereafter abbreviated as GT], (Musoorie: Dalama, 1962), [modern blockprint, 310 folios], ka 48b. 7 ff. Also: Nga-wang-pel-den (Ngag-dbang-dpal-ldan), *Annotations for the 'Great Exposition of Tenets', Freeing the Knots of the Difficult Points, A Precious Jewel of Clear Thought* (*Grub mtha' chen mo'i mchan 'grel dka' gnad mdud grol blo gsal gces nor*) [hereafter abbreviated as Ann.], (Sarnath: Pleasure of Elegant Sayings Printing Press, 1964), [modern blockprint, 416 folios], 101 b. 2 ff.
2. Ann., stod 63b.3.
3. This list is adapted from *Meditation on Emptiness* by Jeffrey Hopkins, (Ann Arbor : University Microfilms, 1973), p. 76.
4. Ann., stod 65a.3.
5. Ann., stod 64b.2.
6. Ann., stod 65a.3.
7. Ann., stod 64b.2; GT, 30b.5; Ann., stod 51b.2.
8. Jang-kya (lCang-skya), *Clear Exposition of the Presentation of*

Tenets, A Beautiful Ornament for the Meru of the Subduer's Teaching (*Grub pa'i mtha'i rnam par bzhag pa gsal par bshad pa thub bstan lhun po'i mdzes rgyan*) [abbreviated hereafter as Jang], (Varaṇāsī, 1970), p. 32.8.

9. Ann., stod 65a.4.
10. Ann., stod 64b.4.
11. Ann., stod 64b.8.
12. GT, ka 42b.8.
13. The author elaborates three different presentations by these three, of which only the second is translated.
14. Jang, 212.17.
15. According to the blockprint edition in the University of Wisconsin rare books room, this passage should read: *de'i 'jug thogs su mthong lam bar chad med lam gyis nyon sgrib kun btags dang/shes sgrib kun btags sa bon dang bcas pa spangs nas rnam grol lam dang 'gog pa'i bden pa gnyis mngon du byed do// sgom lam skor dgus sgom spang nyon mongs bcu drug gi sa bon dang sgom spang shes sgrib brgya dang brgyad kyi sa bon rim can du spong bar gsungs so//*
16. The text mistakenly reads: *sgra gang zag gi bdag med.*
17. The light of the sun and moon is said to close some flowers.

BIBLIOGRAPHY

(The references for the entries marked 'P' are to the Peking edition of the *Tibetan Tripitaka* published by Suzuki Research Foundation, Tokyo-Kyoto, 1956.)

A. SŪTRAS

1. *Descent into Laṅkā Sūtra*
   Laṅkāvatāra-sūtra
   Lang kar gshegs pa'i mdo. P775, Vol. 29.
2. *Perfection of Wisdom Sūtras*
   Prajñāpāramitā-sūtra
   Shes rab kyi pha rol tu phyin pa'i mdo. Vols. 12–21.
3. *Unravelling of the Thought Sūtra*
   Saṃdhinirmocana-sūtra
   dGongs pa nges par 'grel pa'i mdo. P774, Vol. 29.
4. *Sūtra on the Ten Grounds*
   Daśabhūmika-sūtra
   mDo sde sa bcu pa. P761–31, Vol. 25.

B. COMMENTARIES

5. Asaṅga. *Compendium of Knowledge*
   Abhidharmasamuccaya
   mNgon pa kun btus. P5550, Vol. 112.
6. Asaṅga. *Five Treatises on the Levels*
   Yogacaryābhūmi
   rNal 'byor spyod pa'i sa. P5536, 5537, 5538, Vol. 109–10.
   Yogacaryābhūminirṇayasaṃgraha
   rNal 'byor spyod pa'i sa rnam par gtan la dbab pa bsdu ba. P5539, Vol. 110–11.
   Yogacaryābhūmau vastusaṃgraha
   rNal 'byor spyod pa'i sa las gzhi bsdu ba. P5540, Vol. 111.
   Yogacaryābhūmau paryāyasaṃgraha

rNal 'byor spyod pa'i sa las rnam grang bsdu ba. P5543, Vol. 111.
Yogacaryābhūmau vivaraṇasaṃgraha
rNal 'byor spyod pa'i sa las rnam par bshad pa bsdu ba. P5543, Vol. 111.

7. Bhāvaviveka. *Blaze of Reasoning, a Commentary on the 'Heart of the Middle Way'*
Madhyamakahṛdayavṛttitarkajvālā
dbU ma'i snying po'i 'grel pa rtog ge 'bar ba. P5256, Vol. 96.

8. Bhāvaviveka. *Heart of the Middle Way*
Madhyamakahṛdayakārikā
dbU ma'i snying po'i tshig le'ur byas pa. P5255, Vol. 96.

9. Dharmakīrti. *Seven Treatises on Valid Cognition*
Pramāṇavarttikakārikā
Tshad ma rnam 'grel gyi tshig le'ur byas pa. P5709, Vol. 130.
Pramāṇaviniścaya
Tshad ma rnam par nges pa. P5710, Vol. 130.
Nyāyabinduprakaraṇa
Rigs pa'i thigs pa zhes bya ba'i rab tu byed pa. P5711, Vol. 130.
Hetubindunāmaprakaraṇa
gTan tshigs kyi thigs pa zhes bya ba rab tu byed pa. P5712, Vol. 130.
Sambandhaparīkṣāvṛtti
'Brel pa brtag pa'i rab tu byed pa. P5713, Vol. 130.
Vādanyāyanāmaprakaraṇa
rTsod pa'i rigs pa zhes bya ba'i rab tu byed pa. P5715, Vol. 130.
Saṃtānāntarasiddhināmaprakaraṇa
rGyud bzhan grub pa zhes bya ba'i rab tu byed pa. P5716, Vol. 130.

10. Dharmamitra. *Clear Words, a Commentary on (Maitreya's) 'Ornament for the Realizations'*
Abhisamayālaṃkārakārikāprajñāpāramitopadeśaśāstraṭīkā.
Shes rab kyi pha rol tu phyin pa'i man ngag gi bstan bcos mngon par rtogs pa'i rgyan gyi tshig le'ur byas pa'i 'grel bshad tshig rab tu gsal ba zhes bya ba. P5194, Vol. 91.

11. Fourth Panchen Lama, Lo-sang-pel-den-ten-pay-nyi-ma (bLo-bzang-dpal-ldan-bstan-pa'i-nyi-ma). *Instructions on the Three Principal Aspects of the Path to Highest Enlightenment, Essence of All the Scriptures, Quintessence of Helping Others*
gSung rab kun gyi snying po lam gyi gtso bo rnam pa gsum gyi khrid yig gzhan phan snying po. [Place and year of publication unknown]

12. Kön-chok-jik-may-wang-po (dKon-mchog-'jigs-med-dbang-po). *Precious Garland of Tenets* or *Presentations of Tenets, a Precious Garland*
Grub pa'i mtha'i rnam par bzhag pa rin po che'i phreng ba (Yongs-dgon-mtshan-nyid-grva-tshang, no date).
13. Maitreya. *Mahāyāna Treatise on the Sublime Science*
Mahāyānottaratantraśāstra
Theg pa chen po rgyud bla ma'i bstan bcos. P5525, Vol. 108.
14. Maitreya. *Ornament for the Realizations*
Abhisamayālaṃkāra
mNgon par rtogs pa'i rgyan. P5184, Vol. 88.
15. Śāntideva. *Compendium of Instructions*
Śikṣāsamuccayakārikā
bsLab pa kun las btus pa'i tshig le'ur byas pa. P5272, Vol. 102.
16. Tsong-ka-pa (Tsong-kha-pa). *Three Principal Aspects of the Path to Highest Enlightenment*
Lam gyi gtso bo rnam pa gsum. P6087, Vol. 153.
17. Vajragarbha. *Commentary on the Condensation of the Hevajra Tantra*
Hevajrapiṇḍārthaṭīkā
Kye'i rdo rje bsdus pa'i don gyi rgya cher 'grel pa. P2310, Vol. 53.
18. Vasubandhu. *Treasury of Knowledge*
Abhidharmakośakārikā
Chos mngon pa'i mdzod kyi tshig le'ur byas pa. P5590, Vol. 115.

INDEX